LEADERSHIP FOR EVERYONE

LEADERSHIP FOR EVERYONE

How to Apply the Seven Essential
Skills to Become a Great Motivator,
Influencer, and Leader

Peter J. Dean, Ph.D.

McGraw-Hill

New York   Chicago   San Francisco   Lisbon   London   Madrid   Mexico City
Milan   New Delhi   San Juan   Seoul   Singapore   Sydney   Toronto

The **McGraw·Hill** Companies

1 2 3 4 5 6 7 8 9 0   DOC/DOC   0 9 8 7 6 5

ISBN 0-07-145340-7

McGraw-Hill books are available at special discounts to use as premiums and sales promotions, or for use in corporate training programs. For more information, please write to the Director of Special Sales, McGraw-Hill Professional, Two Penn Plaza, New York, NY 10121-2298. Or contact your local bookstore.

This book is printed on recycled, acid-free paper containing a minimum of 50% recycled de-inked paper.

Dedicated to
Isabelle Helen Dean
and
Molly Dickinson Shepard

Contents

PREFACE

Leadership development is essential to the growth and productivity of an individual's professional and personal life. To be successful, pursuing such an endeavor must be a conscious choice that can take two forms and occur everyday if so desired. First, you can approach leadership as a field of study: reading research, considering existing models, and internalizing the standard and established benchmarks of effective leadership. Assess what others have learned about leadership to further your own understanding. There is an abundance of material on the subject available to anyone with a library card, Internet connection, or a nearby bookstore. An intellectual approach increases your understanding of how leadership models have evolved and sharpens your ability to perceive the nuances of authentic leadership. I have used this approach personally and professionally.

A second approach is a more personal one: evaluating your own experiences in your career and personal life to build and strengthen leadership skills. Often I have attempted to apply my knowledge of leadership to a number of posts that I have held, including my time as the Supervisor of Military Intelligence Operations in Munich, Germany, and the position I once held as National Leader for two nonprofit learning centers in Pakistan. *Leadership Development* was actually in my job title when I was the Supervisor of Leadership Development for the Avionics Division at Rockwell International, Inc. in Cedar Rapids, Iowa.

Within all these opportunities for leadership application, I failed more often than I succeeded. Sometimes, the feedback I received about my leadership ability was most unforgiving. When you take the responsibility to interact as a leader, people expect you to lead. And if you do not connect with people as a genuine person of humility, those you lead will share feedback with you that should steer you in the direction of humility. A humble approach and the importance of character development will then become your focus in order to improve your leadership abilities. Imagine if you expected everyone with whom you worked to operate seamlessly together right off the bat without direction and without any problems. Allowing leadership to float among a work group must be approached with a disciplined attitude, as it is not for the fainthearted.

This book is about everyday leadership where individuals find ways to become influencers, mentors, and teachers regardless of title or position, increasing their sphere of influence as they further hone their leadership capabilities. When I started considering the skills of everyday leadership I thought I knew how to lead because I had written a dissertation on the subject and was convinced I knew everything I needed to know. After much effort, I realized a purely intellectual approach did not prepare me as well as I had hoped. I still lacked the actual capacity to practice positive, authentic, and human leadership. I wish I could say I understood this early on, but I did not. It took many failures before I began to look toward what constitutes the successful *practice* of leadership. This gave rise to years of trial-and-error in the essentials of leadership, which I will share later in this book. I can't say that I have mastered the proper leadership method in every one of my interactions, but I do know these methods work when used. These skills can be practiced regardless of your knowledge of leadership literature or your job title. Hands-on practice is the second way one can approach leadership development.

This second approach is easy to understand but challenging to execute and can only be mastered over time if you practice everyday in your actions and conversations. It results in the daily development of leadership capacity. Consistent, successful practice then enables people to have a greater influence in all the spheres of their life, both at work and at home. Also, it prepares the person to accept—and attract—more and more responsibility personally and professionally.

The L.E.A.D.E.R.S. Method™ works for those who make real effort to improve their abilities to lead. I developed this method after recognizing deficits in my own leadership skill base. This method is a testimony to the lessons I have learned in my many years of leadership study and experience.

The seven essentials of the L.E.A.D.E.R.S. Method are as follows:

1. Listen to Learn
2. Empathize with Emotions
3. Attend to Aspirations
4. Diagnose and Detail
5. Engage for Good Ends
6. Respond with Respectfulness
7. Speak with Specificity

This method takes courage, honesty, an ability to keep your own ego needs at bay, and persistent commitment. Practicing this method will lead to success.

I have found success as a leader and I have failed miserably. But I failed much less and caused fewer calamities after I developed and employed this method in my interactions with people. The L.E.A.D.E.R.S. Method not only speaks to the seven essential skills of the everyday leader, it is the beginning point in comprehensive development of everyday human leadership.

LEADERSHIP
FOR
EVERYONE

HOW TO LEAD

INTRODUCTION

The goal of this book is to help you learn how to practice leadership in every situation, regardless of rank or station in life. It will show you how to make every interaction an opportunity to lead. Whether you consider yourself a natural born leader or not, the skills and techniques covered in the following chapters will enable you to lead in whatever situation you find yourself, both in business and outside of the workplace. Leadership can be learned, and the seven essential skills that belie the L.E.A.D.E.R.S. Method will help you develop your leadership abilities. This method has been proven to create *everyday leaders*: individuals who seize the potential in any and every interaction to lead, positively and authentically. So leadership exchanges occur not only with people at the top of the organization, but at every level in between. Leadership can indeed be learned, and like any skill must be increasingly practiced. The goal here is to establish yourself as a leader and continually expand your sphere of influence, so that you become a proactive and effective contributor to any effort or team in which you participate.

Anyone who has a part in the mission of a work system that involves the inputs, tasks, processes, procedures, systems, outputs, outcomes, schedules, deadlines, etc. can take an active role as a leader. These leaders can help fulfill their team's or company's strategic vision, and create a mentoring and non-threatening workplace for their colleagues.

OPPORTUNITIES TO LEAD

Our everyday interactions, whether with our children, partner, or colleagues, present opportunities to lead. Individual leadership moments take the form of influencing decisions, acting as a mentor, or directing a business venture. The ability to harness the power of interpersonal relationships by understanding the dynamic of a particular interaction and then making a deliberate choice about how the interaction should be managed is the hallmark of the method described in this book. Each of the seven skills will help you build on this understanding and capability, which is critical in developing a leader who is not driven by agenda, but embodies the precepts of the authentic leader. These leadership moments will culminate in an environment that is adaptable, supportive, and emotionally stable. Leaders from the shop floor to the boardroom can create a toxic or nontoxic work environment through their day-to-day interactions, resulting in either dissonance and poor results or an enthusiastic environment with records of high performance (Goleman, Boyatzis, McKee, 2002).

Everyday leaders are "quiet leaders," according to Joseph Badaracco, a Harvard professor, who suggests that each day in all organizations, a million seemingly inconsequential decisions are made by these individuals who ultimately reinforce and strengthen a work system's efficacy (Badaracco, 2002). Quiet leaders balance the desire for productivity with a basic trust in humanity, using the character qualities of restraint, modesty, and tenacity in the interactions with others. Similarly, management expert Michael Useem, professor at The Wharton School, in Leading Up: How to Lead Your Boss So You Both Win, suggests that everyday leaders use the qualities of determination, fortitude, and perseverance to add value to the work environment and to exercise effective pursuit of the greater good (Useem, 2001). The skills you will be introduced to in this book create quiet leaders, who are able to confront, analyze, and work through any business challenge and in the process further develop the traits noted above.

If we want to see the results of strong leadership within any work system, we have to let leadership float among all workers. Nearly everyone can lead, whether an entry-level agent or employee, a productive sales advisor, or a vice-president negotiating financial arrangements for the company. Anyone can uniquely position themselves to practice leadership and, through role modeling that creates a safe place for others to lead, they can then develop other leaders.

This book challenges the assumption that only a few can lead and the rest must merely follow. It illustrates the powerful organization wide impact of everyday leaders. Moreover, the book offers the most important lesson for leaders: the value of learning through leading. It provides an understanding of the essential and practical interpersonal skills needed to practice everyday leadership—to be a quiet leader. Although these skills are primarily used in one-on-one interactions, they also are effective in group interactions and even within the larger organizational system. This book provides a new mental model for who or what is a leader, so that the opportunity to practice the precepts of leadership extends to all individuals.

THE L.E.A.D.E.R.S. METHOD

The L.E.A.D.E.R.S. Method contains the essential skills necessary for any effective leader to practice. While these skills are practiced to some degree individually, it is their integration and systematic use that will result in optimum leadership ability. And with more individuals practicing the Method, leadership will be demonstrated at all levels of the organization. L.E.A.D.E.R.S. is an acronym for the seven critical skills, which will be introduced in this chapter and discussed in greater detail in Part 2 of the book. They are:

1. Listen to Learn
2. Empathize with Emotions
3. Attend to Aspirations
4. Diagnose and Detail
5. Engage for Good Ends
6. Respond with Respectfulness
7. Speak with Specificity

LISTEN TO LEARN

Listening results in learning. This has probably been your experience since you were in grade school. But in the workplace, listening takes on an even greater importance than just gaining content knowledge, allowing you to gain insight into your managers and colleagues. Taken to the next level, this insight and deeper understanding will further focus your efforts and that of your team so that you are performing at the highest possible level.

EMPATHIZE WITH EMOTIONS

If you understand the emotional base from which a person is speaking, then you are empathizing with that person and as such are better able to grasp the content as well as the context of his or her message. With this understanding it is easier to act like a leader, reacting with patience, fortitude, selflessness, and fair play.

ATTEND TO ASPIRATIONS

The third step in the Method is to inspire and assist individuals in developing their goals and meeting aspirations.

DIAGNOSE AND DETAIL

It is understood that every individual is made up of their particular past experiences and acquired skills. These factors affect attitude and behavior. When an individual is placed in a work environment, they are affected by specific expectations directly communicated to them; reliable feedback measures; well-proportioned infrastructure where resources, systems, and processes are in place; and non-pay incentives such as recognition and rewards. Once you have all of this in mind, you are then properly prepared to truly understand a person's performance at work. You must objectively weigh the positive or negative effects of the system surrounding the performer against the qualities and experiences they bring to the situation. This big-picture conceptualization greatly clarifies the mission, vision, and standards for performance for an individual within the mission, vision, and standards of the organization.

ENGAGE FOR GOOD ENDS

After you listen to learn, empathize with emotions, attend to aspirations, and diagnose and detail the situation, you are ready to engage for good ends. First you must consider your own intentions, the rules and standards you are projecting, and the desired results of your actions and comments. You too are made up of a combination of your skills, history, and the outside forces that affect your performances as a leader. If you step back and evaluate these factors within yourself, then you will be engaging for good ends to benefit your colleagues and your organization.

RESPOND WITH RESPECTFULNESS

Prejudice and stereotyping create a negative slippery slope in the realm of interpersonal relations. Unfounded preconceptions compromise the personal dignity of others, and will harm your reputation as a leader. Prior to your response to another person, you must keep your eyes open to the possibilities and strengths that every person brings to the table and establish an atmosphere of respect. If you back your words and actions with genuine respect, you are likely to create trust in communication and earn respect in return. Leadership and personal initiative will flourish when everyone on the team feels respected and free to speak and act without prejudgment.

SPEAK WITH SPECIFICITY

Always take careful notice of the words you choose, the sound of your voice, the facial expressions you make, the eye contact you establish, and the body language you employ. These verbal, vocal, and visual components are essential elements of all interactions, and communicate more than any words on a page. When all elements of communication are aligned to express your point, your listener will better grasp your statements. Beware of the distorted or mixed messages you may be sending with nonverbal communication. When you engage, move, and speak with specificity, you will be able to impart a true understanding of your ideas.

Part 2 of the book unpacks these skills and shows you how to apply them as you develop your abilities as an everyday leader. Think of them as building blocks that involve receiving feedback, interpreting that feedback, and then offering an informed response. Certainly, there are more skills that can be added to our list of seven, however, these form the foundation of leadership practice. Creating an open environment that elicits communication, supplying guidance from your own base of experiences that involves introspection and self-disclosure, and offering useful, positive, and supportive feedback in return are all necessary talents of a successful leader. As we drill down further into the L.E.A.D.E.R.S. Method, you will see how the seven skills fall into three categories:

- Listen to Learn—→Receiving Feedback
- Empathize with Emotions—→Receiving Feedback
- Attend to Aspirations—→Receiving Feedback
- Diagnose and Detail—→Assessing and Analyzing
- Engage for good Ends—→Giving Feedback
- Respond with Respectfulness—→Giving Feedback
- Speak with Specificity—→Giving Feedback

The chapters that follow will deliver the mental models, tools, and words for self-leadership. And perhaps this is an ability that is prized more than ever in modern business, where the organizational structure is lean. Companies who operate as lean, agile organizations need leaders at every level, but rarely instruct their workforce as to what this actually means or how to go about achieving it. Before we discuss how each skill is learned and applied, let's explore what it means to be an everyday leader.

C H A P T E R

2

THE EVERYDAY LEADER

LEADERSHIP HELD HOSTAGE

The literature on leadership for the past century focuses mostly on leadership from the role of a hero leader, using traits, functions, style, station in life, position in a system, or many followers. Ronald Heifetz sheds insight on this interpretation in his book, *Leadership without Easy Answers* (Belknap Press), which discusses four models of leadership: trait, situational, contingency, and interaction of leader and follower. Heifetz recognizes that all four approaches support the value of influence over outcomes—that is, "how to control others." The models define leadership as a means of gaining and keeping influence over constituents as the leader rises in prominence and power. This is the leader as controller. He suggests that the practice of leadership must expand beyond those with legitimate positions of authority, and forego the labels of leader and follower. When relationships are reciprocal, leadership emerges in the communications of both participants.

This approach holds that the practice of leadership is not held hostage by positions of authority or stature. Leadership begins to be practiced at all levels of the organization, where individuals act within their sphere of influence without being labeled as leaders. I also believe that everyday leaders can simply lead within their "sphere of influence" at work and at home in one conversation at a time. Heifetz supports my notion of everyday, everywhere leadership indirectly at the end of his book, where he states:

> Leadership takes place every day. It is neither the traits of a few, a rare event, nor a once-in-a-lifetime opportunity. In our world, in our politics and businesses, we face adaptive challenges all the time. Every time we face a conflict among competing values, or encounter a gap between our shared values and the way we live, we face the need to learn new ways. Leadership ... requires a learning strategy. A leader has to engage people in facing the challenge, adjusting their values, changing perspectives, and developing new habits of behavior (Heifetz, 1998).

The opportunity for practicing everyday leadership is fueled by the speed of change. Our global society is experiencing an ever-increasing rate of change in the categories of technology, economics, politics, social factors, knowledge, and systemic thinking. There is change within these categories, and because of the interaction and crossover between categories, the expectation is that the rate of change will continue to increase.

In their 1999 work *Everyone a Leader*, Horst Bergmann, Kathleen Hurson, and Darlene Russ-Eft speak cogently about what has created the opportunities for more people to practice more leadership. They propose the following:

1. The traditional structure of organizations is changing from formal to cross-functional and long-distance in response to the competitive need for "better, faster, cheaper, and newer." The modern organization, they say, is a "fishnet"—strong, resilient, and flexible enough to change drastically depending on the forces upon it from the customer and the organization.

2. Because of the change in the formal structure, there are fewer managerial ranks, and the existing managers are

busier delegating responsibility and doling out projects, not managing the routine.

3.   The percentage of knowledge workers—the people who analyze data to create information and use that information—has increased more than any other category of workers in all occupations, according to the U.S. Bureau of Labor Statistics. These workers are more self-managing but may not be self-leading (Bergmann, Hurson, Russ-Eft, 1999).

A recent survey of 347 Senior Executive Service members (Abramson, Clyburn, Mercier, 1999) indicated that adaptability and flexibility are the key leadership attributes for facing future change, accountability for results, and visionary and strategic thinking. Everyday leaders must support the efforts of honest and competent people to find solutions to problems. Thus, to be effective, leaders must strive to develop the leader in everyone.

To ascertain the necessary qualities of leaders, James Kouzes and Barry Posner asked people to complete a checklist of the characteristics they looked for and admired in a leader in their book, *The Leadership Challenge*. The results of the survey are shown in Table 1.

In virtually every survey, honesty has always ranked first. Forward-looking and competence also have received votes from a majority of respondents. Honesty, forward-looking and competence are the three most important elements of credibility, which everyone can practice both everyday and everywhere.

A recent interview of 21 federal executives who received the Presidential Distinguished Executive Rank Award in 1997 also highlights the importance of honesty and competence (Huddleston, 2000).

These high-performing individuals were asked about the secrets to their success. The responses included these four key ingredients:

1.   They each have a clear strategy for their agency.
2.   They strive to animate other people.

3.   They work hard.

4.   They have integrity.

It cannot be overstated— overall, honesty and competence are the foundation of all working relationships, and of all relationships that work.

The Kouzes and Posner survey pointed out that effective leaders must be forward-looking, have a sense of direction, and show concern for the future of the organization. They should be energetic and positive about the future, and able to communicate their ideas in ways that uplift and encourage others to help. They must point people in pioneering directions, and instill energy and drive into those around them. The

TABLE 1. TWENTY MOST DESIRABLE
CHARACTERISTICS OF LEADERS

Rank	Characteristics
1	Honest
2	Forward-looking
3	Competent
4	Inspiring
5	Intelligent
6	Fair-minded
7	Broad-minded
8	Supportive
9	Straightforward
10	Dependable
11	Cooperative
12	Determined
13	Imaginative
14	Ambitious
15	Courageous
16	Caring
17	Mature
18	Loyal
19	Self-controlled
20	Independent

Source: Kouzes, Posner (2002).

strongest leaders get people focused on and enthusiastic about building the organization for the future by putting today's actions in a strategic context. When added to that crucial foundation of honesty and competence, these qualities and practices result in authentic leadership. And anyone, anywhere in a work environment can possess these characteristics. It is another reason why everyday, everywhere leadership is possible in today's workplace.

CHANGE AT WORK INVOLVES EVERYONE— EVERYONE CAN LEAD

The difficulty of any change is that it is likely to be extremely complex, and is certain to tax the attention, intelligence, powers, and will of anyone interested in initiating and managing transformation.

Change requires an honest articulation of fresh visions of the future. Those visions do not necessarily have to come from the top of the work system. To implement a vision there are seven specific strategies that everyday, everywhere leaders can use to improve performance:

1. *Embrace external accountability.* This is one of the most important strategies.

2. *Modify the organizational work.* It is essential for the everyday leader to redesign the structure of work to suit the needs of the organization or agency.

3. *Establish internal accountability.* To implement new ideas, the everyday leader must raise the level of internal accountability.

4. *Gain additional resources.* Success in realizing a new vision depends not only on doing more with available resources but also on trying to gain necessary new resources.

5. *Undertake major, publicized initiatives.* The everyday leader must stimulate the organization to become more innovative. This can be accomplished through widely publicized initiatives to increase organizational confidence and spur ongoing improvements.

6. *Reengineer basic operational procedures.* The successful
    everyday leaders must diagnose and heal any internal
    turmoil within the organization's basic operational pro-
    cedures.

7. *Encourage co-production and responsiveness.* To achieve
    sustainable organizational change, the everyday leader
    must recognize the organization's clients not only as
    recipients of services but also as an important part of the
    production processes. Decentralizing leadership practice
    and spreading it throughout all levels helps to build a
    working partnership among members in the organiza-
    tion—the everyday, everywhere leaders in the work sys-
    tem. This enables all members to self-lead.

In *True Success: A New Philosophy of Excellence*, Tom Morris
suggests the following as a way of self-development through
self-leadership. His thoughts are in harmony with my notion
of everyday leadership:

> It is not impossible for everybody to be a success. Set-
> ting high goals is not necessarily a matter of striving to
> become a company president. Stretching yourself does-
> n't have to mean increasing your income, fame, power
> or social status. It means digging deep into your own
> heart, finding what you are capable of and not settling
> for anything less. It means … exercising and enjoying
> every aspect of who you are … and walking that path
> everyday (Morris, 1994).

In preparation for mastering the seven essential skills for
the everyday leader and instilling desirable characteristics of a
leader into a work system, you ought to be able to set aside
your personal preconceptions in order to be open and receptive to other people. You must have a Personal Me vs. Interpersonal Me conversation with yourself. This internal
conversation allows the individual to frame interactions without making incorrect assumptions such as:

- If I practice these everyday leadership skills, I will receive grand approval from co-workers, peers, and managers right away.
- Promotion and pay raises will result immediately.
- I am the only one practicing these skills.

If you are beginning to use the L.E.A.D.E.R.S. Method with those notions in mind, it is the wrong way to start. You must begin with the primary goal of self-development. Perhaps, after you master the skills, the material benefit will occur. Perhaps it will not. What you gain is the long-term development of your individual character and integrity. That is what leadership development ought to be about.

THE PERSONAL ME VS. INTERPERSONAL ME DECISION

Everyday leaders find opportunities every day to develop as a leader in their own "sphere of influence." They make a choice between the personal me, who may want to have the courage to grow and expand their talent and skill base, and the interpersonal me, who may want to be accepted, comfortable, and safe in interactions with others. Leader development is self-development. It encourages peer development as well, enabling everyone in the work environment, either on a project or a team, to develop their skills as leaders. A group of colleagues who all act as everyday leaders creates a culture of productivity. Direction floats from member to member, as when a single member temporarily takes the lead with the better idea. Here, positive and progressive ideas emerge organically, without force.

THE PERSONAL LEADER: INDIVIDUAL
DEVELOPMENT OF THE PERSONAL ME

Individual development requires the ability to develop a self-concept. Self-concept is each person's unique package of attitudes, habits, perceptions, and drives. Being open to unpacking the self to understand it better requires courage and character. That openness is half the challenge. Any leader must understand that he or she plays many roles in life: father, mother, husband, wife, businessperson, academic, citizen, nature lover, museum buff, etc. Self-concept is actually a combination of many different self-concepts, stemming from the many roles we play in our society. Because people are required to wear many hats in life, conflict is likely to occur between certain responsibilities, perhaps resulting in less than effective performance in one or more roles. If you take time to reflect on the potential conflicts between your multiple roles, you will come to better understand the dynamics of each. If you do not process this incongruity, others on the job may see you differently than you see yourself, or differently than you would like to be seen. This disparity can result in acts of ineffective leadership. If the everyday leader's self-assessments are pragmatic, however, the remedy for conflict is easier than you might think. Simply work to develop a more realistic and accurate self-concept. Individuals who succeed at self-development take time to examine and to truly understand the nature of the conflicts among their many roles. They can then more objectively comprehend their performances in each of these roles, and how their behaviors affect other people. As their self-concepts become more integrated into their daily thoughts and actions, leaders gain new energy and insight.

Paul Brouwer (1964) suggests the following sequence of actions to enable an individual to understand and thus realize an integrated self-concept:

- *Self-examination.* Everyday leaders know there is always more that they do not know about themselves, or are aware of the areas in which they require improvement. Questions about oneself are seeds of change, and they may lead to eventual changed behavior. The inquiries themselves are the catalyst for self-development. (In Part 2 of this book, we will examine the general categories of essential behavioral skills, and how to recognize them in yourself and in others.)

- *Self-expectation.* Everyday leaders set their sights on every possible positive and progressive change they can transform into reality. Each new insight elevates the bar of expectation. In essence, you must accept that you have had limited influence in the past, and you are now ready to do something about it.

- *Self-direction.* When everyday leaders have examined themselves and raised their expectations, they increase their self-knowledge. Soon they are overcoming their own obstacles, and performing well on the job and elsewhere. Self-learning is so powerful that it makes one become very motivated to keep the growth moving forward. It helps everyday leaders gain the intrinsic knowledge that they are worthwhile, they have recognized that their voice is being heard, and they now know they can affect positive and progressive changes in all parts of their life.

- *Self-management.* Self-management enables everyday leaders to balance the many demands of their life, stemming not just from playing several conflicting roles, but also from demands on physical, mental, emotional, and spiritual capacity. Self-management requires good nutrition, maintaining a healthy weight, proper rest, physical exercise, time with family, work and social balance, intellectual growth, appropriate outlets for emotion, application of virtues, a sense of humor, and individual spirituality. This sort of self-management is hard work, and requires a balance and blend of the components of personal development and actualizing what you learned from exploration of the personal self. Personal development on this level is further challenged if your self-image is not aligned with how other people perceive you. Success in all of these areas leads not only to everyday leadership, but an overall sense of contentment.

It is at this point that everyday leaders have the answers to many questions about the value of their lives, what to do with it, and how to be themselves. From there, they can address their personal goals. This has an added benefit for the work environment. The positive influence of the everyday leader inspires others to find their own innate motivation on the job.

THE INTERPERSONAL LEADER: WHERE CHOOSING
SELF-DEVELOPMENT MEANS FOCUSING ON OTHERS

Part 2 of this book explains the specific mechanics of the seven skills of everyday leadership. The power of the process depends on your own personal development—that is, as mentioned earlier, to handle your internal personal stuff and set it aside in order to be receptive to others. One must do this regardless of how threatening or confusing another person's communication may be. Thus, practicing the L.E.A.D.E.R.S. Method has a lot to do with the skills of the personal leader. It is essential to put your self-concept aside. This allows everyday leaders to understand the messages they receive and enables them to respond objectively. Afterward, the everyday leader can retrieve his or her personal self-concept without its having been damaged or lessened in any way, with confidence intact. The foundation of the seven essential skills for everyday leaders is the ability to effectively manage emotions and tendencies.

THE L.E.A.D.E.R.S.
METHOD

3

LISTEN TO LEARN

Listen to Learn, one of the seven interpersonal skills, best illustrates the fundamental elements available for use in any conversation. As suggested above, prior to conversations with co-workers, managers, reporters, friends, and family, it is helpful to adopt the mindset that your interactions are not tainted by agenda, ego, or emotions—what I call managing your "personal self." With your personal self contained, you can relate to others with greater openness. Once this skill has been developed, it will begin to have a dynamic effect on subsequent conversations and increasingly valuable exchanges will emerge and increase in number. To reach this level of interaction, it is, above all, important to *listen*. To have a complete understanding of the context of the interaction, you must Listen to Learn.

EXAMPLES OF LISTENING TO LEARN

The most obvious example of listening to learn is in broadcast journalism. Every morning we see Katie Couric or Matt Lauer in interviews with public figures from business, politics, and entertainment, and we witness skilled reporters arranging a set of questions, asking those questions, and analyzing the answers that come back to them. They must put aside their own subjective thoughts and objectively discover and report whatever it is they can learn about the story they are covering. They are Listening to Learn, and the more successful they are as news analysts means the more successful they have been in keeping their own biases outside of the interview. Listening to Learn can be seen when a professor is listening to a student or a parent is listening to a child while learning exactly where the person is in their development in order to customize the dialogue to further that development.

Yet it is in the workplace—in business—where we spend the majority of our time and where it is most important to practice this skill. As a leadership consultant for 30 years, I have often observed that if a manager is liked it is usually because he or she first listens and then incorporates that information into subsequent decisions, immediately validating the views of the person who had the exchange with the manager in the first place. In his book *The World's Most Powerful Leadership Principles* (2005), James C. Hunter refers to a Gallup Organization study which shows that more than two-thirds of people who quit their jobs do so because of an ineffective manager. In these cases, people are quitting their manager, not their organization. These examples of Listening to Learn underscore the value of practicing temperance, patience, and fortitude, particularly in a workplace setting. The next sections further define this skill and suggest dialogues, tools, and tactics for practicing it effectively at every opportunity.

WHAT IS LISTENING?

Carl Rogers summarized psychotherapy as a way to deal with a failure in communication. Miscommunication had more serious consequences for Paul Newman's character in the movie *Cool Hand Luke*, who was subjected to the cruelty of a prison warden who neatly summed up Luke's problem with the line, "What we have here is a failure to communicate." Thankfully, Rogers had a more reasonable and less barbaric remedy to the problems of miscommunication than did the prison warden character, recommending "active listening."

> Active listening [where one senses accurately the feelings and personal meanings the other person is experiencing] is exceedingly rare in our lives. We think we listen, but rarely do we listen with real understanding....Yet, listening is one of the most potent forces for change I know (Rogers, 1980).

In business perhaps more attention needs to be paid to listening rather than to other components of communication. The payoff for true active listening is rewarding positive and progressive success. Active listening is collaborative and comprehensive. It is listening with purpose, hearing what is being said, recognizing tone of voice and mood of the person speaking, having an open mind, and avoiding distractions. Of the seven skills, listening is the most important one for successful exchanges.

In many settings, learning is achieved through listening. In the business world, both listening and learning are prerequisites for leading. Although it is commonly accepted that listening to learn is valuable, we rarely receive direct instruction on its value. One of my greatest frustrations in consulting in the private and public sectors is the amount of time, energy, and talent wasted when people in positions of power talk excessively and listen for their own words to bounce back to them from others. This is costly in terms of time, but more important, the person who is speaking is losing opportunities to learn from other's expertise and experiences. How very sad that we believe that people in positions of power are supposed to talk more, when in actuality, they are the ones who should be listening the most. Hearing and understanding the message that the other person actually sends, and not planning what to say when it is your turn to talk is successful, active listening.

ACTIVE LISTENING LEADS TO ACTIVE TWO-WAY LEARNING

In the last few pages we have established that at its best, listening is an active skill, not a passive state of mind. It takes effort to be an effective listener. To be an active, non-defensive, listener requires such personal strengths as self-restraint, courage, honesty, perception, and willingness to receive feedback. To be a good listener you need to embody generosity, discernment, and good judgment about what to say and how to say it. We also have to be mindful of our attention wavering as well as unintentionally tuning out the content of the speaker's message. A good listener gives and solicits feedback in a two-way learning mode, where the "pause" becomes a great listening tool. These pauses allow the listener to accommodate the speaker and assimilate the knowledge or content that precedes the pause. Active listening does not mean waiting for your time to talk when someone else is speaking and not listening to what that person is saying. It means making an honest attempt to hear and understand what is being said and putting it into the public arena of joint understanding. This allows learning to occur for both persons, and the conversation becomes a true exchange of understanding.

Active listening also involves sending a visual message to the other person underscoring that you are paying attention to what is being said. You can convey this by making eye contact with the person who is speaking and by exhibiting other nonverbal behavior. One suggestion is to model the other person's nonverbal behavior. If she smiles, you smile back. If he nods, you nod back. If she looks interested in the topic, you make your expression mirror back her interest. In their book *The Handbook for Leaders*, John Zenger and Joseph Folkman (2005) comment that when listeners respond with negative expressions to all speakers, not making eye contact with the person or mirroring back their expression, on a widespread basis within an organization, great damage to that company is likely caused.

LISTEN TO LEARN VERBALLY, VOCALLY, AND VISUALLY

Listening only really happens when we receive the verbal, vocal, and visual components of a message and attempt to align the components for clarity. If we listen only to the words, we might miss the fact that the sender's visual message contradicts the verbal message. In other cases, the sender's tone of voice may obscure the words. Visual cues may suggest that the words we are hearing may not be the whole story.

WHY LISTEN?

There are at least five advantages to listening:

1. As discussed, we can learn from others by listening.
2. Listening gives us time to codify our thinking.
3. Listening leads to problem solving.
4. Listening helps us to make better decisions.
5. Effective listening gives us the self-confidence we need to begin practicing everyday leadership and further hone our decision-making skills.

WHAT ENABLES LISTENING TO LEARN?

Here are some characteristics of those who Listen to Learn:

- Self-awareness and self-regulation
- Intellectual capacity: maturity, ability, conviction
- Emotional capacity: readiness, willingness, attitude
- Courage to hear conflict as creative energy
- Willingness to deal with problems
- Ability to work toward a joint understanding of the message

The task of conversing is complicated by the filters we bring to that conversation. Those filters, which interfere with communication, are based on the past experience of the sender and receiver. Such filters include language, memories, values, attitudes, style, beliefs, information, knowledge, feelings, and emotional capacity, to name a few.

When the sender encodes the message and delivers it, he or she has to be aware of the receiver's past-experience filters, which help or hinder the receiver to decode the message. The listener must also accept some responsibility for attempting to assure a two-way learning experience.

Some research suggests that individuals process 40 bits of information every second (Csikszentmihalyi, 1990). Those same people have an upper limit of processing 126 bits per second. Therefore, it is easy to see that if individuals could put their own thoughts aside, they could understand much more than 40 bits of information per second. One thing is certain, most people fall far below their peak capacity to process what someone else is saying. Active listening can increase that capacity by creating the space for accommodating and assimilating information.

Usually, most of us can assimilate thoughts two or three times as fast as it takes someone to convey a message. For example, an individual probably is able to speak at about 125 words a minute but thinks at a rate four times faster. That is a large discrepancy between speaking and thinking. That extra thinking time is an important concept and good news to those who want to practice effective listening. We can either choose to focus fully on what is being said, or we can concentrate on what the other person is saying only every now and then. Letting the mind wander in and out of the conversation leads people to jump to conclusions. Creating space in the conversation for accommodating and assimilating the information, however, is critical in the skill of listening to learn.

True listening or focusing completely on what is being said—both the actual text and the subtext of the message—requires great willpower, especially since human nature seems to push us to hear only what pleases us and reject what does not. Also, we all have a range of interest and if a topic is outside that range, we have a tendency to resist the ideas. To be an active listener, however, we must be able to avoid discarding ideas that differ from our own. This does not mean we have to abandon our personal likes and dislikes, but we do have to suspend them when we are assimilating the message. Fortunately, there are some secondary skills that can help us Listen to Learn. For instance, one way to keep the mind from wavering during a conversation is to check our understanding of what is being said by asking questions—for example, "As I understand it so far …," or "Do you mean this …," or "Let me be sure I understand …." This facilitates accommodation and assimilation of the speaker's information and intention.

WHAT PREVENTS ACTIVE LISTENING?

Information overload is one common cause of poor listening. Even though today's youth seem to be able to handle multiple stimuli better than earlier generations, I am not sure we should rely on that multitasking experience to train us to be better listeners.

A lack of openness and trust on the part of the person speaking also affects listening ability. (This will be discussed in greater detail in Chapter 4, Empathize their Emotions and Chapter 5, Attend to Aspirations.) Moreover, cultural differences, even subcultural differences within a city, can prevent good listening. (We talk about this in detail in Chapter 8, Respond with Respectfulness.)

Sometimes we are distracted while listening by getting caught in the sound of the person's voice, either pleasurable or irritating. At other times, we may be distracted by the person's mannerisms. At still other times we may be searching for evidence to support what is being said. A lack of confidence in our own ability to isolate key ideas from a myriad of details sometimes derails active listening. It is better to glean the patterns or themes of what is being said and ask questions later to fill in the details. Or we may just be in an uncooperative, resistant mood and really not available emotionally or intellectually to Listen to Learn. It is good to remember these things when it seems someone is not listening to us.

Other barriers to effective, active listening include:

- Lacking self-discipline
- Lacking objectivity
- Becoming overemotional about the topic
- Listening only for facts
- Missing the effect of the speaker's tone of voice or the visual part of the message
- Faking attention
- Mentally evading certain parts of the message
- Responding to emotional words
- Having a limited vocabulary
- Listening only for the next time you can speak
- Attacking the speaker's credibility
- Asserting your own opinions that might be contrary to the speaker's
- Worrying about defending yourself
- Being afraid the speaker will dominate you in the conversation
- Expecting the speaker to think and feel as you do
- Trying to keep the upper hand to maintain your security
- Thinking that every conversation must have a winner and a loser
- Expecting the speaker to respond to whatever communication problems develop
- Being uncomfortable with allowing the speaker to know you too well

Dr. Karl Menninger once remarked that listening is a magnetic, strange, and creative force (Hunter, 2004, p. 117). The person we gravitate toward is the one that listens to us. So many people pay large sums of money to therapists primarily so someone will take the time to listen to them. It seems what is referred to as the "talking cure" in psychology is really more a "listening cure" that anyone can practice. To this point, Robert Greenleaf (1977) once said that true listening builds strength in other people, so we forget about being interesting in order to satisfy our own ego, and focus on being genuinely interested. Without true listening, we send the message that we are not able to empathize with another person. If the other person recognizes that we are truly listening, that person will know that we are genuinely empathetic. (Empathy is discussed in Chapter 4, Empathize their Emotions.)

Years ago, as a consultant to the Unisys Corporation, the company's new name after the merger of the Sperry Corporation and Burroughs Inc., I learned from an executive at Sperry the company's take on the interpersonal skill of listening. The Sperry Corporation introduced a seminar in 1979 which offered instruction in good listening habits. The response was positive, and it seemed that Sperry employees wanted to spend more time developing these habits. Sperry then launched a corporate advertising campaign promoting the value of good listening. J. Paul Lyet, Sperry's Chairman and CEO, strongly believed that in order for the seminars and the advertising to be completely effective, listening had to become part of Sperry's business philosophy.

According to Sperry's research, listening is the most used of four basic workplace skills (before speaking, reading, and writing) but the least taught. Studies show the average listener retains only half of what is said in a 10-minute presentation and within 48 hours, retention drops off by half again. At best, only 25 percent of what is heard is understood, properly evaluated, and retained. What is worse, as Sperry saw it, was that ideas were commonly distorted by as much as 80 percent as they travel through the many levels of an organization. Developing a depth of skill in active listening at Sperry became a central part of individual development. The four categories of listening they spoke about in the 1980s are still relevant today.

The four general categories of listeners, with each category reflecting a varying level of attentiveness and sensitivity on the part of the listener, are described in the next several sections.

FOUR GENERAL CATEGORIES OF LISTENING

At one time or another, we each fall into one of the four categories of listening:

1. Inattentive listening
2. Selective or marginal listening
3. Critically evaluative listening
4. Active listening

The key to achieving active listening is to be aware of when we are being too critical, selective, or inattentive, and then adjust our effort as needed during the course of the conversation.

INATTENTIVE LISTENING

Inattentive listeners prefer to be speaking. It is likely while someone else is speaking they are simply thinking about the next area of conversation they jump into. They may adopt blank stares as well as nervous mannerisms, and they usually fake attentiveness. Social conversations hold their attention more than business conversations, and they become more attentive listeners if the content is emotional or related to feelings. While the credibility of the speaker increases their attentiveness, they may interrupt the speaker often. They organize information around their own need for social recognition and popularity as opposed to organizational concerns or task accomplishment. The basic personal skills of temperance, patience, and fortitude are limited, thus, the interpersonal skill of listening to learn is also limited.

SELECTIVE OR MARGINAL LISTENING

Selective listeners hear what their thoughts, ideas, and opinions lead them to hear. They, too, have trouble with the personal skills of temperance, patience, and fortitude. Because of this lack of self-management, they skim the surface of the conversation and never risk going any deeper. They prefer to postpone problems rather than deal with them. If the conversation attempts any depth, selective listeners will find a distraction, as they prefer to evade difficult or complex situations and usually listen only for the bottom line or the main ideas. If the message addresses their ego, they are likely to be better listeners. They organize information around egoistic pursuits. They'll consider a plan if the goal or task fit into their egoistic needs.

CRITICALLY EVALUATIVE LISTENING

Critically evaluative listeners seek logic, order, and proof. Their focus is on only the details of what the speaker is trying to say; they make no effort to understand the speaker's intent. Critically evaluative listeners are more concerned about content than feelings which may prevent them from seeing the big picture. Also, they form opinions long before the speaker has been able to relay the entire message. These listeners organize information around the content or task at hand, not the feelings of the person speaking. There are times when this mode of listening is very valuable, but it is even more powerful if used in tandem with active listening.

ACTIVE LISTENING

Active listeners are the most functional, involved, and patient listeners whatever the subject matter. These listeners demonstrate their respect for the speaker verbally, vocally, and visually, and show real empathy for what the other person is trying to communicate and how he or she feels about it. Active listeners are able to place themselves in the speaker's position, see their thoughts and feelings from the speaker's point of view, and align thoughts and feelings to those of the speaker's. They listen for both the intent and feeling of the message.

Active listeners organize incoming information around the person speaking. This does not mean that these listeners are overly gullible or too easily persuaded. They actively listen and then critically diagnose the information before making any decisions. Practicing effective, active listening takes work and must be done in tandem with the remaining six interpersonal skills in the L.E.A.D.E.R.S Method.

HOW TO LISTEN TO LEARN

As I mentioned earlier, there are a number of secondary skills and tactics that can be used to be an effective listener. Tips for more effective active listening are to:

- Maintain consistent eye contact.
- Face the speaker.
- Avoid distractions.
- Make listening your primary focus; don't multitask.
- Wait until the speaker is finished before formulating a response.
- Don't interrupt; use this as an opportunity to learn.
- Assess the whole message (verbally, vocally, and visually).
- Identify and reduce filters that block the information.
- Suspend judgment but look for the worth of the content.
- Communicate your attention verbally and nonverbally.
- Use pauses and silences in the conversation constructively to absorb what the speaker has said and respond appropriately.

    Also, it is important to avoid the following traps:
- Criticizing the delivery
- Convincing yourself the content is not interesting
- Faking attention
- Responding as if you are just barely tolerating the content

ADDITIONAL LISTEN-TO-LEARN PRACTICES

Additional methods that enhance your understanding of the speaker's message include:

- *Clarify the message.* To get additional facts or to help explore more sides of the topic use questions such as these: "Can you explain this to me a little further?" "I understand this part, but help me understand more clearly." "Why is this issue important to you (alternative: … at this time)?"

- *Restate the message.* To verify the speaker's meaning and your interpretation of the message, as well as to show that you are interested in understanding what is being said, it is a good idea to pause the conversation for a summary statement. For example: "As I understand it, your plan is …" "These are the points you have suggested that I understand so far …" "This is what you have decided to do …"

- *Encourage the message.* To convey that you are interested in what is being said and how the speaker feels about the content, make comments designed to explore the issue further, such as: "You feel upset at that behavior?" "You felt you were not treated fairly?"

- *Justify the message.* To help the speaker evaluate his or her own message, make statements such as these: "That is very interesting. What other aspects are involved?" "Are these the keys ideas you want me to understand?"

- *Summarize the message.* To enable the speaker to bring the discussion into focus and to possibly use as a springboard to additional discussion, you might ask, "These are the key ideas I have heard you express. Am I right?"

In his book *Human Relations in Business*, Keith Davis (1957) lists guides for successful, active listening that include:

1. Stop talking.
2. Put the speaker at ease in a permissive environment.
3. Look and act interested to show you want to understand.
4. Remove distractions, shut the door, seek quietness.
5. Put yourself in his or her place.
6. Be patient and allow plenty of time.
7. Hold your temper as anger gives the wrong meaning to words.

8.   Go easy on argument.

9.   Ask questions.

10. Stop talking again.

LEARNING DURING LISTENING IS ALSO LEADING

It is helpful when developing your ability for active listening that you make certain assumptions. Listening within this context will more greatly enhance your skills as a leader.

1.   *Each person has a unique learning style.* Some learn best by reading, others by doing, still others by discussing or listening. All will benefit by taking action in any way they can.

2.   *Each person learns at a different rate.* Hence, some may be confused or lost in early stages. It is okay not to get it the first time you hear it. Try to be patient with yourself and others.

3.   *Each person learns different things from a common experience.* Be open and encourage trading perceptions and accepting different feelings and views.

4.   *Each person learns best from his or her own experience.* Testing other ideas against your own situation helps us learn. A healthy skepticism toward any one "best way" to process change in organizations is an effective way to Listen to Learn.

Two of the most useful powers you possess as an everyday leader are your powers to listen and observe. It is said that the Almighty gave us two ears, two eyes, and only one mouth for a reason. We were meant to listen and observe at least twice as much as we speak. Listening and observing both require empathy and active attentiveness to the speaker.

John F. Kennedy believed that learning and leading are indispensable to each other. Listening to Learn is one of the most fundamental leadership skills; two other interpersonal skills, Empathize their Emotions and Attend to Aspirations, enhance this skill threefold.

4

EMPATHIZE THEIR EMOTIONS

Practicing the personal skills of the virtues of temperance, patience, and fortitude as well as practicing the skill of Listening to Learn lay the foundation for the second skill in the L.E.A.D.E.R.S. Method: Empathize their Emotions. Having set our own agenda and emotions off to the side, we can focus on the goals and the emotional state of the person speaking. Recognizing the speaker's effect apart from your own enables you to empathize with the speaker's needs, goals, and attitudes.

EMPATHY

In explaining the work of Carl Rogers, Morley Segal defines *empathy* as aligning your feelings *with* the person, not feeling sorry for the person (Segal, 1997). Feeling sorry for the other person, or feeling sympathy, implies a sense of the speaker's helplessness, which may diminish the value of the interpersonal communication. Sympathy makes it harder to have a genuine conversation and causes a loss of objectivity. Empathy creates a sense of openness and an acceptance of all attitudes or emotions. It is the ability to pick up on the thinking and feel-ings of the other person. Empathy also keeps us from evaluating or judging the other person, which blocks real communication, and that, in turn, helps us respond better. One obstacle to empa-thy is the inability to change our perception of someone else; that is, to hold on to a preconceived idea of the person. Empa-thetic feedback will clearly present a different perception of the same person.

It is important to realize that empathy is a powerful tool that must be used genuinely if it is to support authentic leadership. In their book *How to Hire and Develop Your Next Top Performer: The Five Qualities That Make Salespeople Great*, authors Greenberg, Weinstein, and Sweeney go so far as to suggest that empathy is amoral; that people can use empathy without good ends in mind or to service their own selfish needs (Greenberg, Weinstein, and Sweeney, 2001). Yet empathy can also be used to help persuade someone to make a right decision. Ethics must be used with empathy, which is why the next interpersonal skill, Engage for Good Ends, is among the seven skills practiced by true leaders.

EMOTIONS

In one of their several books on the subject, Daniel Goleman, Richard Boyatzis, and Annie McKee (2002) identify four domains of emotional intelligence:

1. Self-awareness
2. Self-management
3. Empathy
4. Social and relationship management

Self-awareness is the ability to recognize and understand moods and intentions or drivers, and self-management is the ability to control and redirect these attitudes in order to arrive at your goals. These components are a necessary part of your personal preparation before an interaction takes place. Social and relationship management refers to the skills of being politically savvy by creating and maintaining healthy relation-ships within the organization.

Everyday leaders must be able to put aside their judgments, biases, preoccupation with self, preconceived ideas, and emotions to perform well in their sphere of influence, all the while without putting themselves at the mercy of the other person. If communication stalls, it may become necessary to use questions and statements to keep the conversation going in a productive way. Periods of silence help too, allowing for important self-evaluation to take place.

POSITIVE AND NEGATIVE REACTIONS

We all experience positive and negative thoughts. Knowing this reinforces the importance of empathy as a skill to manage one's attitudes and emotions positively and productively. Even if you believe that someone is being unrealistic and unreasonable, it's important to ferret out something positive and true in your exchange and work with that part of the communication for good ends. To truly influence your sphere of contact, you must acknowledge the other person's feelings, whether you share them or not, and use your exchange to both resolve those emotions and further the goal or task at hand.

Dealing with and resolving negative emotions have a remarkable effect on your ability to lead. First of all, it is one of the most compassionate efforts you can make on another person's behalf. Also, it helps the person experiencing the negativity to calm down. Once the person is calm, you can begin a more positive dialogue, using the person's own words to paraphrase your understanding of what he or she is experiencing. Everyday leaders who do this help to create a warm, supportive, and understanding culture in their personal sphere of influence.

IT HELPS TO KNOW ABOUT EMOTIONS

There are hundreds of emotions that individuals at all stations of life must deal with daily. Daniel Goleman lists the eight most frequently experienced emotions: anger, sadness, fear, enjoyment, love, surprise, disgust, shame (Goleman, 1995, 289–299). Within these basic categories of emotion, there are subcategories as shown below.

1. *Anger:* fury, outrage, resentment, wrath, exasperation, indignation, vexation, acrimony, animosity, annoyance, irritability, hostility, hatred, and violence
2. *Sadness:* grief, sorrow, cheerlessness, gloom, melancholy, self-pity, loneliness, dejection, despair, and depression
3. *Fear:* anxiety, apprehension, nervousness, concern, consternation, misgiving, wariness, qualm, edginess, dread, fright, terror, phobia, and panic
4. *Enjoyment:* happiness, joy, relief, contentment, bliss, delight, amusement, pride, sensual pleasure, thrill, rapture, gratification, satisfaction, euphoria, whimsy, ecstasy, and mania
5. *Love:* acceptance, friendliness, trust, kindness, affinity, devotion, adoration, and infatuation
6. *Surprise:* shock, astonishment, amazement, and wonder
7. *Disgust:* contempt, disdain, scorn, abhorrence, aversion, distaste, and revulsion
8. *Shame:* guilt, embarrassment, chagrin, remorse, humiliation, regret, mortification, and contrition

These eight categories of emotions represent what we potentially deal with in our everyday conversations. Although recognizing these different emotions is critical to effective leadership skill, it is often not focused on adequately.

Moods are different than emotions; moods last longer. Temperaments, too, are different from emotions; temperaments evoke a mood or a given emotion. Disorders of emotion, moods, and temperaments, such as depression or anxiety represent perpetual states that last much longer. When dealing with emotions, moods, temperaments, and disorders, we are not dealing in the land of logic; nor do emotions emerge from the rational mind. However, the rational mind can control the reaction to an emotion or mood. Goleman contends that we do not decide with the mind when to be sad or happy, but we can be aware of the emotion and regulate it (Goleman, Boyatzis, McKee, 2002).

HOW WE USE THE SKILL

When everyday leaders practice Empathizing Their Emotions, they first recognize, either from what is being said or perhaps through facial expression and body language, an emotion, reflect on that emotion in a nonthreatening way, and facilitate a discussion that should ensure the person his or her feelings have been understood. A good leader then moves to the content of the conversation in a way that will address, ease, or resolve the emotion.

For example, everyday leaders recognize emotion by bringing it into the conversation to show that they understand. This also demonstrates that they are Listening to Learn. Effective approaches for achieving a level of empathy that both parties recognize include remarks like these:

- "Help me understand why you are so concerned about this."
- "You seem very concerned about this. Why?"
- "Is there some concern that may cause some ill feelings between us?"

Furthermore, empathizing emotions helps to encourage feedback and to create a work atmosphere where disclosure by others can occur more easily.

Techniques that communicate your understanding of the other person's feelings include:

1. Tuning out distractions.
2. Identifying the feelings you think others are experiencing.
3. Probing to reveal what caused these feelings.
4. Responding with comments as described above.
5. Letting the other person clarify if needed.

It is always a good idea to have two-way communications on all issues in the workplace. Each conversation thus becomes a building block of trust and fortitude. Even though it is a comedy, the movie *Office Space* depicts the emotional abuse to which employees are subject in the course of a day. It also shows (perhaps in an extreme example) how counterproductive it is to adopt an abusive way of communicating. The negativity exchanged among members in an organization is a daily occurrence. Ineffective, one-way, mocking communication displaces productivity in every conversation and results in a loss of efficiency and civility in the workplace. In fact, workers see rebellion as a positive reaction to the oppression they are experiencing.

The everyday leader with the interpersonal skills of listening and empathizing lays the groundwork for truly attending to the aspirations of the individual who is speaking. We will discuss this more fully in the next chapter.

The skill to Empathize their Emotions includes but is not limited to the following approaches:

- Seeking to know the area of emotional stress—work, family, health, money, values, personality.
- Seeking to know the emotion itself—alienation, boredom, anger, apathy, bashfulness, depression, envy, discouragement, fearfulness, frustration, hopefulness, helplessness, pride, jealousness, humiliation, shock, suspicion, withdrawal.
- Reflecting their emotion to empathize their emotion.
- Paraphrasing your understanding of their emotion and the underlying concern or issue.
- Beginning the discussion of the content that was overshadowed by the emotion.

5

ATTEND TO ASPIRATIONS

Expanding the interpersonal practice of the first two skills requires an understanding that the nature of life is to grow and develop. Attending to Aspirations recognizes that every person has a natural penchant to grow and develop. If we are forced by organizational structure or managerial power to accept limitations on our innate ability to grow and develop, it can be quite damaging to leadership development. Management oppression and low expectations thwart creativity and leadership as first noted in Douglas McGregor's seminal work on the topic, *The Human Side of Enterprise* (McGregor, 1960). This management style tends to stall individual growth under the justification of efficient and effective productivity. I have seen that setting limitations on individuals actually brings about lower on-the-job productivity. Over time, these limitations cause people in the workplace seeking growth and individual development either to leave the company or regress to performing mediocre work. Allowing for individual members of a work team to develop their ability is self-actualizing and helps achieve the goals of the company. Individual aspirations can bring about great improvement in company productivity, and developing leadership abilities in employees shows managers that their reports are committed to the business and reflects the company's commitment to its employees. Attending to Aspirations, the natural tendency in each of us to grow and develop, is a powerful, productive, and positive force at work, although it is a resource of many companies that is hardly tapped.

One of the greatest frustrations is seeing people who work for a living having their aspirations to grow thwarted by others. It is almost as if the members of an organization become institutionalized and lose their own developmental compass. This sets up such a negative spiral of dissatisfaction, within which people can only lose their drive for growth and productivity at work. The people who have not been damaged too severely, simply quit, impacting the performance levels and quality of work coming out of the firm, not to mention the reduction in organizational knowledge.

A number of famous psychologists defined the ability to grow and develop as an individual in terms that have informed my own definition of the process. Piaget (1973) described the tendency to grow as the process of an active mind developing its human knowledge. Freud (1917; Strachey, ed., 1963) recognized it in the three universal growth forces of the subconscious—instinct (id), morality (superego), and reason (ego). Jung (1964) called it an inherent drive to grow and develop in a life-long quest for meaning. Jung saw the nature to grow as a way of removing neurotic thinking and feeling. He suggested that not being allowed to understand the reality of psychological phenomena is one reason for the failure to adapt to growth. Fromm (1941) called it people's freedom to experience themselves through the embodiment of their powers, whereby they can be productive. This is not possible in a totalitarian state dominated by an authoritarian character, which is how management is often perceived.

Rogers (1959) called it a self-actualizing tendency toward a fully functioning personality in the basic human condition. He puts the responsibility and control for this growth on the individual. Horney (1950) called it an inner force, common to all human beings and yet unique to each, which is a deep source of growth. Lewin (1947) referred to it as the expansion of personal life space, where we reduce the constraining forces opposing growth and increase the driving force of growth. Lewin's perspective was from a systems view of the interaction of the parts (individual) and the whole (environment) and how that interaction helps or hinders progress.

And finally, Goleman, Boyatzis, and McKee (2002) called it primal leadership, where a leader creates emotional resonance in relations with others so all members may grow. Anyone who wants to be an everyday leader should create the same resonance suggested by Goleman, Boyatzis, and McKee. The result will be a positive atmosphere that primes the reservoirs of the best in people and allows for mutual growth.

One aspect that all these impressive thinkers agree on is that growth is natural. And like anything natural or instinctual, these tendencies can be stunted by an environment that is oppressive. Knowing this, it is important to discuss the things that everyday leaders can do to foster the natural tendency to grow and develop in spite of unforgiving environments. Primarily this involves acting as a leader in their own sphere of influence, cultivating a productive work environment one conversation at a time.

SO, WHAT ARE ASPIRATIONS?

Aspirations are the motives that drive us to act. They are generated from within. While some inner aspirations spur us to actions as clear as hunger and thirst, we are not always aware of these motivations. As I have said previously, it may be our own ego gratification that spurs us on to be productive without true concern for the specific task or people involved. Authors Greenberg, Weinstein, and Sweeney in their work, *How to Hire and Develop Your Next Top Performer: The Five Qualities That Make Salespeople Great* (2001), suggest that if there are internal aspirations for good ends and concern for joint understanding, and if the external environment does not inhibit but, rather, enhances them, people will be productive because they feel secure that the culture at work supports growth and development. An aspiration can also be described as a strong desire or ambition for advancement or progress in life. Aspirations exist in our professional lives and our personal lives. If our aspirations in the work system—our inner drives that cause us to act—are allowed to emerge, these aspirations will benefit the company, too.

All individuals have aspirations—visions of themselves in the future. Everyday leaders know that attending to aspirations is important because it helps others grow. With that growth comes a better working condition and a better culture. Individual aspirations are important to recognize and understand; doing so will make the individual happy and more productive. However, individuals in positions where they cannot realize those aspirations or they are not being clear about what those aspirations are, productivity and morale will go downhill.

WHAT PREVENTS ATTENDING TO ASPIRATIONS?

Unfortunately, sometimes an organization's values are not always clear. The behaviors of the leaders and members of a company are not always in alignment with the values and mission of the organization. This was clear in the scandals of Enron, Tyco, WorldCom, Anderson, and Adelphia. Everyday leaders can slowly change a company's culture by acting in ways congruent to its vision, mission, and values as that action is in alignment with their values as well. Behaviors are typically based on what motivates an individual. If individuals' values are not aligned with the organization's, employees will not be motivated to reach their own goals and aspirations; nor will they be motivated to reach those of the organization. It is clear, then, that an organization must be explicit about its vision, mission, and values so that individuals can express their personal aspirations.

Another obstacle that prevents us from knowing others' aspirations is not understanding their level of need. Each person operates from his or her own level of need. Everyday leaders can identify this need if they Listen to Learn, Empathize Their Emotions, and Attend to Aspirations.

MASLOW'S HIERARCHY OF NEEDS

In his hierarchy of needs within which individuals can reach self-actualization, Abraham Maslow (1943) demonstrated the importance of understanding the needs of others. This hierarchy describes what motivates us as individuals from lowest needs to highest needs. Maslow did not intend to suggest that these were independent levels of need, only that there is a general progression that takes place through the various levels. Maslow's lower-order needs begin with the physiological needs, which include food, drink, and sex. When these needs are gratified, other higher needs begin to emerge. For most of us, the higher needs are stronger because, generally, we are not in situations that deprive us of our basic physiological needs.

The next level of needs is our safety needs. Again, many of us feel safe in our surroundings because of the efforts to stay away from criminals, extreme temperatures, tyranny, and so on. The next two levels of needs in the hierarchy relate to love and esteem. Love needs include love, affection, and belongingness. If the physiological and safety needs are primarily satisfied, naturally we feel the need for love, for companionship. Note, however, that love is not synonymous with sex, which is a physiological need. Love is more the feeling of belonging in a place in a group that makes you feel important.

Esteem needs relate to a desire for a certain reputation and prestige. Most important, we want respect from others based on our achievements. If these needs are satisfied, we have feelings of confidence, strength, and worth. When love and esteem needs are satisfied, people move to the highest-order need of self-actualization.

Self-actualization relates most closely to understanding people's aspirations. Even if all of the other needs are satisfied, if individuals are not doing what they enjoy or feel fitted for, they will be discontent. This is the need to become more than we are; to be self-fulfilled. Unfortunately, not many people reach this stage, primarily because there are so many other needs in their lives that they do not reach a point at which they can identify what will fulfill them.

In their book *Don't Waste Your Talent,* authors McDonald and Hutchenson describe how individuals hit "turning points" (McDonald and Hutchenson, 2000). Turning points are times when individuals reflect on their lack of fulfillment at certain points in their lives and feel the need to change, although, often, they do not know how to make that change. They remain stagnant and do not move to the level of self-actualization. However, it is much easier to reach a level of self-actualization if there is a high degree of communication. The more people who know individuals' motivations and aspirations, the more likely these individuals are to reach the desired level of self-actualization because of the support and encouragement they receive.

> It is important to recognize that these needs, although in a hierarchy, are not fixed. That is why it is important to attend to others as individuals and not make assumptions about their motivations and aspirations as if they are the same for everyone. Maslow explains that highly self-actualized people, like everyday leaders, assimilate their work into their self-identity. Clearly, if everyday leaders are aspiring toward their goals of growth and development, and are increasing their capacity for responsibility and higher-level work, and if they have the right environmental factors (such as clear expectations, proper and timely feedback, appropriate resource allocation, and honest pay and nonpay incentives), their work will be part of their self-identity. They will then be likely to be highly motivated to achieve the goals of the organization because their own goals will be congruent to those of the company.

EXPECTATIONS AND SELF-ACTUALIZATION

Self-actualization is linked to the expectancy theory originally developed by V. H. Vroom (Vroom and Yetton, 1973). Self-motivation at work affects the overall effectiveness of the work itself. Porter and Lawler (1968) developed a theoretical model, expanding on Vroom's original concepts that people make decisions and choose actions based on their perceptions, attitudes, and beliefs. Two concepts that everyday leaders can use to keep a positive perception, attitude, and belief system at work are as follows:

1. People need challenging work goals commensurate with their skills, knowledge, education, training, and experience. Typically, nonchallenging work results in frustration and boredom. Overly challenging work that exceeds the current skill level leads to frustration, dissatisfaction, and defeat.

2. Trust must be established among members of the organization. Everyday leaders need to follow through and believe that others will follow through on promises. This requires honesty and openness. Fairness is critical too. Constructive feedback is required in order to develop leadership among members with open and tactful communication.

HOW TO ATTEND TO ASPIRATIONS

Before practicing everyday leadership, consider the following questions:

- What level of ability does this person display?
- What education and experiential background does he or she possess?
- What are this person's interests, goals, values, and beliefs?
- What motivates this individual?
- What is the person's level of need?

People do not always produce at work because organizational structure—the systems and processes designed by managers—sometimes squash individual workers' creativity and innovation in trying to grow and develop as they accomplish their job. In an exclusionary environment, it is easy for individuals to go about their jobs without aspiring to make themselves or situations better. However, with a more participatory environment, individuals are free to make suggestions, to create, and to make decisions for themselves. This enhances their feeling of self-worth, their drive for self-actualization, and their aspiration to reach their goals.

SUCCESS IS BASED ON THE COMMITMENT OF EVERYDAY LEADERS

For members of any work system to do a good job, they need feedback, support, and room for self-determination. Often, it is much easier for an organization to provide an extrinsic reward of some kind and not focus on the intrinsic motivators of their members. Getting organizations to change, however, is not the primary focus of this book. The emphasis here is that everyday leaders can concentrate on the person, irrespective of the structure.

Everyday leaders help others to set the goals so both parties are more willing to work together to achieve them and are less resistant to change. Understanding expectations and setting goals together—goals that are realistic and in accordance with skills and abilities—helps optimize performance and achieves organizational targets. Approaching objectives in this way enhances the relationship between all involved, increases motivation, and in so doing, the work itself takes on increased meaning. Feedback that attends to an individual's aspirations intensifies the meaningfulness of tasks and responsibilities. In addition to making the work environment more significant, feedback that supports an individual's growth and development strengthens productivity and performance.

FEEDBACK MOVES US FORWARD

Delivering feedback in a way that it can be received without threat or insult by the other person is not an easy task. This ability requires practice in both developing sensitivity to other people's needs and being able to empathize with the other individual. Some people feel that giving and receiving feedback cannot be learned solely by practice, but first requires internalizing the basic philosophy that individuals must be accepting both of themselves and others. As this acceptance of self and others increases, the need to give feedback that can be construed as judgmental decreases, and giving nonthreatening feedback becomes an easy-to-use technique— a true conversational exchange.

In order to effectively communicate feedback, certain behaviors must be avoided. William James spoke of this in his *Talks to Teachers on Psychology and to Students on Life's Ideals*, published in 1899. He states that "errors of excess" and "blindness to needs of others" have a negative effect in conversations and productivity (James, 1899; reprnt, 1983). Excess occurs when loyalty becomes fanaticism or love becomes possessiveness. These exaggerations of apparent virtuous qualities turn out to be a quest to derive pleasure from our own need for self-satisfaction. When any positive quality is expressed in its extreme form, it can diminish the person of that very quality. These errors of excess stem from a blindness or lack of awareness, and they usually emerge in relationships with others where there is an inability to understand one another. If we presume we know what is best for others and what they need, we fall into the error of not recognizing the needs and values of others or their inner reality. This blindness destroys the positive influence on another person in your sphere of influence.

GUIDELINES FOR GIVING AND RECEIVING FEEDBACK

Guidelines that will enhance both giving and receiving feedback and make the communications more effective include the following advice.

GIVING FEEDBACK
1. *Accept yourself and others.* Give feedback that will not be construed as evaluative or judgmental.
2. *Readiness of the receiver.* Give feedback only when the receiver is ready to be aware of it. Otherwise the receiver will be apt not to hear it or will misinterpret it.

3. *Be descriptive, not interpretive.* Give a clear report of the facts. It is up to the receiver to consider the reasons or meanings or to invite feedback from the speaker.

4. *Give feedback immediately.* The closer the feedback is to the time the event took place, the better. The receiver is most likely to be clear on exactly what is meant.

5. *Give feedback at appropriate times.* Feedback should be given when there is a good chance that it can be used constructively. It may not be helpful if the receiver feels there is other work that currently demands more attention. Also, be aware that critical feedback in front of others may be more damaging than helpful.

6. *Don't state the obvious.* There is a tendency in giving feedback to say only the obvious. Consider whether what you are reacting to is really new information for the receiver. Often, what is helpful to the receiver is not just a report of what you saw the receiver doing, for example, but the impact it had on you— the way it caused you to feel or the situation it put you in.

7. *Give feedback only about things that can be changed.* Feedback can lead to improvements only when it is about things that can actually be changed.

8. *Do not demand change.* Giving feedback is *not* requesting a person to change. It is up to the receiver to consider whether or not he wishes to change on the basis of new information. It is not helpful to say, in effect: "I have told you what is wrong with you, now change."

9. *Do not overload on feedback.* When we first start to give feedback, we sometimes tend to overdo it. Give concise feedback at a time when the receiver can really act upon it, rather than a long list of items.

10. *Share additional information that might help.* Consider your own reasons for giving your reactions as an everyday leader. If your reasons go beyond simply trying to help the receiver with feedback, you should share these additional reasons so he or she will better understand what you are saying.

11. *Don't patronize.* When giving feedback to a person whose position in the organization's hierarchy is lower than yours, be careful not to patronize, as he or she might feel that you are giving this feedback speaking from perfection. The exchange can often be kept in better balance including some of your own feelings and concerns. Showing that you are not giving feedback for ego-inflating reasons is important. You need to make sure you are not letting your ego interfere with your objectivity. In fact, you might want to get feedback about your feedback.

RECEIVING FEEDBACK

1. *State what you want feedback about.* Let the giver know specific things to which you would like him or her to react.

2. *Check what you have heard.* Check to be sure that you understand what the giver is trying to say. Because the topic is your own behavior, you may tend to think about the meaning of the feedback before you hear it as it was intended.

3. *Share your reactions to the feedback.* Your own feelings may become so involved that you forget to share your reactions to whether or not the feedback has been helpful and how you feel about the person who gave it. The giver needs your reaction about what was helpful and what was not so he or she will know how to improve the ability to give you useful feedback.

4. *Utilize feedback for improvement.* Consider the feedback and try to apply it in specific situations.

5. *Beware of destructive feedback.* Destructive feedback is evaluative, judgmental, preaching, moralizing, admonishing, commanding, or demanding.

The first three essential interpersonal skills of the everyday leader are set forth in the L.E.A.D.E.R.S. Method. The first three skills—Listen to Learn, Empathize Their Emotions, and Attend to Aspirations—are practiced primarily in a receiving mode of a conversation. These three skills allow the optimal amount of information to be received.

One good example of someone using these three skills well is the conversation that Senator Hillary Clinton had with my sister, Reverend Charlene Dean Robbins, about the loss of her son and my nephew, Thomas Robbins, in a munitions explosion in Iraq. Senator Clinton listened to learn about the situation and my sister's perception of the incident, she empathized with my sister with genuine concern, and she attended to the questions of how my sister was dealing with the loss and what changed for her about the loss. There was no request for party support, and there was no fault-finding against the military or the administration. According to my sister, it was a genuine conversation with someone who devoted nearly 45 minutes just to her and her situation.

The dual use of feedback skills in the third interpersonal skill, Attend to Aspirations, serves the fourth interpersonal skill of the L.E.A.D.E.R.S. Method: Diagnose and Detail. This skill takes us into a more cognitive mode. It involves sorting out all the information we gathered using the first three interpersonal skills.

6

DIAGNOSE AND DETAIL

Once we understand the value of listening to learn, empathizing with the person's emotion, and attending to an individual's aspirations, we see that being an everyday leader has more to do with understanding people than imposing our will on others. If you are using these three skills, you are not centered on yourself but on the person to whom you are talking. It is possible to use all of those skills at the same time or to use one more than the others as the conversation progresses. Everyday leaders are able to use these skills by switching off all negative thoughts and feelings about the other person, focusing on what is being said, and eliminating their own interpretation of those same words. Everyday leaders avoid the temptation to interrupt or to react to emotionally loaded words, which usually lead to wrong assumptions and result in undesirable conclusions. Also, the avoidance of interruption and reactions allow for the use of feedback skills. These skills are important to practice before and during diagnosing and detailing the facts in the conversation.

EXAMPLES OF DIAGNOSING AND DETAILING

An example of diagnosing and detailing is Erin Brockovich's righting the wrong of a huge company, even though no law firm dared do it. Her victory was a victory for all everyday leaders. It illustrates the importance of diagnosing and detailing facts in order to discern truth and achieve fairness.

The actions of Lowell Bergman of *60 Minutes* and Dr. Jeffrey Wigand are another example of diagnosing and detailing. Here, two honorable everyday leaders worked together to reveal unethical and illegal practices in the tobacco industry and took a stand against that industry. Making an ethical stand is discussed in Chapter 7, which explains the interpersonal skill Engaging for Good Ends.

Diagnosing and Detailing are critical for successful exchanges in everyday leadership. The mechanics of diagnosing and detailing follow.

PERFORMANCE IMPROVEMENT AT WORK DEPENDS ON DIAGNOSING AND DETAILING

After everyday leaders uncover as much information as possible about an individual's aspirations, they can begin to sort out the details of performance. If we assume that most prefer to perform well rather than poorly at work, we must understand the basics about performance. A person who is serious about improving performance wants to reduce the gaps between an existing state of performance and a better performance. In other words, everyday leaders seek out knowledge at work that will help support their goals and reduce the obstacles that prevent them from being realized. This adds value to our leadership development and organizational goals.

Our performance has two parts to it: the behavior or activity and the outcome or the accomplishment of the behavior. We measure performance in terms of its timeliness, quality, and cost. The behavior or activity of our performance is measured as a cost. The outcome, result, or accomplishment is measured in terms of timeliness and quality. The accomplishment adds value, but the activity or behavior adds cost. In diagnosing and detailing performance, behavior is often confused with accomplishment. Or people see behavior as the performance without ever recognizing the need for an accomplishment to result from that behavior. Behavior that leads to accomplishment equals performance. Understanding this is an important diagnostic advantage if we want to improve our performance and help others improve theirs. The key is to focus on the accomplishments, isolate the gap between what is expected and what is observed, and make changes in the behavior to improve the accomplishment.

Behavior	Accomplishment
What is seen at work	*What is seen after work*
Input, Process, Means	Output, Outcome, Ends
Talking with a customer	Customer satisfaction
Marketing a product	Closed sales
Designing a building	Completed building
Being energetic	Assignments completed early
Evidencing trust	Reporting own errors
Taking the initiative	Fast problem solution

DIAGNOSTIC QUESTIONS TO UNCOVER AREAS THAT NEED MORE DETAIL

Accomplishment should be the object of discussions that diagnose and detail information during conversations with peers at work. Here are two questions that might help the everyday leader identify an accomplishment.

1. Is this what is left after the behavior has ceased and the worker has left the scene?
2. Is this the end purpose of the job, task, or function?

If the answer to both questions is yes, an everyday leader applies the following three criteria of an accomplishment.

1.   Is it measurable?
2.   Is it observable?
3.   Is it reliable?

Categories of accomplishment measures include:

•   Quality (accuracy, class, and novelty): Example, a positive review of a product
•   Quantity (rate, time, and volume): Example, the length of time it took to create it
•   Cost (labor, materials, and management): Example, the total cost of production

The information related to the quality and quantity in the above example can be used as feedback regarding the effectiveness of the performance. Everyday leaders can then incorporate that information in a conversation to help a peer improve activity or behavior, which improves the product or accomplishment.

The second criterion of an accomplishment is that it must be observable if it is to be measured. Examples include:

•   Production time in terms of hours, days, weeks, and months
•   Number of hand-offs of the product
•   Net sales per month
•   Number of repeat customers

Using actual numbers and not fanciful projections is always desirable when diagnosing and detailing.

Establishing reliability is the third criterion for a true accomplishment. This can be gained through two or more independent observers. If they agree regarding the measures of an accomplishment, the everyday leader most likely has accurately identified an accomplishment. If disagreement exists, then the everyday leader should reexamine the job accomplishment, function, or team by returning to the observations. Of course, this probing for detail should occur with tact, temperance, fortitude, and prudence.

Thus, performance is a combination of behaviors and the results or accomplishment the behavior produces. To improve performance an everyday leader must figure out if the accomplishment is valid, measurable, observable, and reliable.

However, that is not the whole story. Behavior is also a function of the interactions between the person and the environment of the work system. In other words, what we as everyday leaders do, feel, perceive, think, and communicate is a function of what the person brings to work and what the environment provides at work. This is a basic principle of psychology and of common sense about everyday leadership. Behavior that is not in touch with the reality of the workplace is abnormally psychotic. An old saying captures this well: Neurotics, who probably make up a larger part of any population, build castles in the air and get depressed when they realize that the castles are only imaginary, whereas psychotics build castles in the air and then move in. Neither of these perspectives is productive in the world of work today. Normal everyday leaders build ideas and seek to accomplish them.

Being able to identify the particular behaviors and accomplishments that represent performance (such as listening, empathizing, or attending) is essential for everyday leadership. This means eliminating the abstract from communication and focusing on the specific. The ability to diagnose and detail behavior plus accomplishment equals performance at work can exist at all levels of an organization. Each everyday leader can help in the process.

There are six levels of diagnosis:

1. Philosophical level: the ideals under which the work system operates
2. Cultural level: the larger environment in which the work system exists
3. Policy level: the missions that define the purpose of the work system
4. Strategic level: the plans designed to carry out the mission
5. Tactical level: the specific duties that achieve the strategies

6.   Logistical level: the support system that enables the
      members to carry out duties

Everyday leaders ask the following questions in looking
for details:

- What is expected?
- What is observed?
- What are the differences?
- What are you willing to do?
- What are you able to do?
- What feedback do you need?
- What information do you need or want?
- What kind of support would enable you to work better?
- Is there enough time to do it right?
- Is equipment appropriate?
- Is allocation of resources appropriate?
- What pay and nonpay incentives are there?
- What are the training needs?
- What are the electronic support system's needs?

OTHER THINGS YOU NEED TO KNOW
ABOUT DIAGNOSING AND DETAILING

Let's face it: There are times in our communication with others
when we have opposing points of view. The skill is to reveal
freely that you disagree but to do so without personal malice.
You should not rely on others to pick up subtle gestures of disagreement. Be direct. The person hearing your opinion should
not feel it is a criticism of him or her but a critique of the content.
That promotes acceptance of the criticism on an intellectual
rather than a personal basis. Disparate opinions should be presented logically showing a clear reasoning process. The beginning point of solving a problem is diagnosing and detailing.

Ask questions in a way that avoids negative responses or
worst yet, makes the person retreat into silence. More than just
questioning techniques are necessary. There also has to be a

framework for the questions to allow for issues of complexity, emotion, motivation, and ability to emerge. The framework for probing the details and some guidelines to observe in that framework, which was originally derived from expectancy theory, developed in the 1980s by Interact, and from my own research for the International Society for Performance Improvement, are shown below.

HOW TO PROBE FOR DETAILS WITHIN EACH LEVEL OF DIAGNOSIS

Guidelines to probe for details include the following:

1. *Discern what is expected and what is observed.* Everyday leaders communicate in a specific and nonthreatening way to obtain information about or open a discussion on a given topic. Being specific is a matter of describing your opinion, perception, or expectation and explaining what you observed that seems to be different from that. Communicating what is expected and what is observed reveals differences in a neutral way; no judgment is rendered and no blame is directed at anyone.

2. *Question without being threatening.* All the "w" questions (what, where, why, when, and who) and the "how" question are useful for everyday leaders, as long as they are not conveyed in a critical, sarcastic, or mocking way. That puts the other person on the defensive. Coming across in a punishing or threatening way may create new problems of understanding rather than lead to an understanding of the current one. The easiest way to avoid this is to focus on conversing about the content in a respectful manner. Chapter 10 deals with ways of Responding with Respectfulness. For now, suffice it to say that labeling the person as lazy, undependable, or sloppy are judgments or projections and tend to cause new problems in communication. Being specific and nonthreatening allows you to delve into the details of the content.

3. *Reinforce what you want to happen again.* Everyday leaders
    see more than only problems in Diagnosing and Detail-
    ing. They also see people who are performing in an
    above-average way, those who have been consistently
    reliable, and those who have met unusual goals or
    expectations. Everyday leaders notice such accomplish-
    ments and positively reinforce them by calling attention
    to them. Examples of positive reinforcement are commu-
    nicating what you observed and describing how it
    exceeded expectations, explaining how the conse-
    quences brought about a positive result, and identifying
    the personal qualities or values that lead to the achieve-
    ment. It is important to reward the action with a simple
    thank you or a show of appreciation.

4. *Make sure you and the other person are ready, willing, and
    able to have the conversation.* When everyday leaders seek
    a joint understanding of the true meaning of the content
    in a conversation, they must check both sides of the
    communication. Start with yourself. Are you Listening
    to Learn? Are you Empathizing their Emotion? Are you
    Attending to Aspirations? Are you asking questions or
    making statements that create a positive atmosphere? If
    your self-check is satisfying, you might want to consider
    if the other person has some "noise" in his or her side of
    the conversation that blocks understanding. Ask your-
    self if you are dealing with a motivation or an ability
    problem. In other words, is he or she unwilling to listen
    or unable to listen?

5. *Ensure that the consequences are clearly understood.* If there
    is a motivational problem—that is, the person is simply
    unwilling to engage in a real dialogue—and it is critical
    that he or she understand, it is good to remember the
    saying, "You can lead a horse to water, but you can't
    make it drink." This means that you can't rely on sheer
    force to motivate. Be aware of what you want to accom-
    plish. You are probably not going to change people's
    values or opinions about the content of the conversation.
    But you can make them aware of the consequences of

poor understanding. People will try to understand the importance of your conversation based on what they think will happen as a result. They are motivated by consequences to them. If you are encountering a problem in communication with someone, point out the consequences that will result if he or she does not understand. These consequences could be related to a task, to others involved, to still another person. Often, just beginning to relate consequences seems to help clarify the conversation, as if hearing consequences put the person into a different frame of mind. Once this happens, you can convey how the understanding will affect the future and move on in the conversation. If pointing out consequences does not seem to foster better understanding, observe your own behavior once more. Check your use of the interpersonal skills Listen to Learn, Empathize Their Emotions, and Attend to Aspirations.

6. *Align yourself verbally, vocally, and visually to the message.* Remember this: What you say accounts for only 7 percent of what they believe. Your vocal tone accounts for 38 percent of what they believe. Last, what you look like when you speak accounts for 55 percent of what they believe. We may be unwittingly sending mixed messages because our facial expressions belie our tone of voice or our words. Mixed messages may account for others' unwillingness to be part of the conversation. If we are receiving mixed messages, we can ask questions to clarify. Ideally, we will have been able to assimilate most of the information by practicing the first three interpersonal skills, but we can also monitor the verbal, vocal, and visual alignment throughout the conversation. That is why listening and observing are so important.

7. *Make sure the person understands what needs to be done.* If there is a problem in Diagnosing and Detailing in a communication, it may be that the person is willing but unable to converse successfully. Then the everyday leader might be able to help him or her by asking for the

person's ideas while listening and observing carefully to determine where the inability may be. Asking another person's ideas not only gets more information but it also invites diversity of information, which helps to arrive at a better decision if a decision needs to be made.

8. *Probe for chronic problems.* Probing is useful if you want more information for the public arena. For example, you could say, "Help me gain more insight about this topic." Or you could ask, "Is there anything else that I need to understand about this topic?"

9. *Deflect sudden changes in emotion.* Sometimes, there is a sudden emotional shift in the conversation, where such negative emotions as anger, frustration, doubt, skepticism, and sarcasm emerge. Everyday leaders handle sudden emotions by simply recognizing them and deflecting them to the speaker. If you ignore the emotion or overreact to it, it makes the other person's emotion escalate. Calmly addressing it sends a reassuring message to the other person that you care and are indeed listening. This action subsequently calms him or her down. As I suggested earlier, you could say: "Help me understand why you are so concerned about this." Or "You seem very concerned about this. Why?" Or you could ask, "Is there some concern that may cause some ill feelings between us?"

10. *Paraphrase complexity.* Sometimes complexity gives rise to emotion. The more complex the conversation, the more likely it is to become emotional. There is a temptation in many of us to deal with the complexity of a topic first and to ignore the emotion. Exactly the opposite is the way we should deal with it. Address the emotion first, then deal with the complexity. Reduce the complexity and then confirm your joint understanding. Paraphrasing—stating what you do understand and asking for more information on what you do not understand—is one way to reduce the complexity of a topic.

The 10 subskills of Diagnosing and Detailing help the everyday leader determine the root causes of blocks in communication and put both speaker and listener on the road to joint understanding. Demonstrating the skills of Listening to Learn, Empathizing Their Emotions, Attending to Aspirations, and Diagnosing and Detailing builds a positive rapport for human decency at work.

The everyday leader can enhance this relationship by using the skill of Engaging for Good Ends. This improves the chances that any outcome arising from the mutual rapport will have an ethical influence in each person's sphere of influence and bode well for the ethics of the organization. This is the topic of Chapter 7, Engage for Good Ends.

7

ENGAGE FOR GOOD ENDS

As everyday leaders interact with others, unseen modes of thinking in decision making may occur that can set the conversation's trajectory on a less productive and/or unethical path. Consciously combating such modes of thinking helps create an atmosphere where the rights of all members are represented—this is where Engaging for Good Ends emerges. At the very least, being an advocate for ethics and professional integrity will mean that you will not be tainted by any unethical practices of others in your organization that may exist.

There is a wonderful story that was told to me by a fellow traveler. Let us call him John. John once had the opportunity to ride in the same limo with Henry Kissinger, President Richard Nixon's secretary of state. This occurred well after the events that caused President Nixon to resign. John knew he would probably only be allowed to ask one question, so he wanted to make sure it was a good one. He simply asked Mr. Kissinger, "Why were you not indicted along with so many of the Nixon administration?" Kissinger's answer was simple indeed and yet very profound. He said, "I was not invited to those meetings." How very exciting that answer was. He was not invited to the meetings where unethical and illegal acts were planned because they knew he would not abide such goings-on. But if you are invited to such meetings in your company, does that mean the company is testing you?

THREE ENEMIES IN THE WORKPLACE

Each of us has a right to think and act in our own self-interest. While this is true, it does not reflect the depth of one's responsibility, and it is certainly not the thinking and action of an everyday leader. If we made decisions solely on the basis of self-interest, it would legitimize opportunistic behavior and, at extreme, result in illegal activities such as theft and fraud. Thus, although our self-interest is important, someone else's is just as important. The self-centered, selfish person who pursues his or her own interest at the expense of others does not give others their due and is the opposite of a just person. Any leader who pursues only profit lacks a requisite sense of justice. Egoism and relativism lay waste to justice at work.

EGOISM
Ethical egoism might be seen as the standard by which businesses operate in a free market system. The noted economist Milton Friedman claimed that the only obligation of a business to society is to increase profits. This thinking follows the egoist view. Yet a society made up of ethical egoists would be dominated by opportunistic behavior. Because ethical egoism legitimizes opportunism, it may lead to actions that bring harm to other human beings. Rejection of ethical egoism doesn't mean an adoption of altruism. What it does mean, however, is an acceptance that there is a nonegoistic foundation for judging right and wrong.

Another critical misconception is that there are no universal standards by which to make decisions. This flaw in decision making emerges from the acceptance that any practice performed by another is permissible because there is no set of universal standards by which to condemn or condone that practice. There are universal principles based upon fundamental human rights such as life, liberty, and the pursuit of happiness.

RELATIVISM

Ethical relativism takes the position that there is no one universal standard or set of standards by which to judge an action's morality. Relativists who defend such a position argue that local custom makes it mandatory that international firms follow local rules. At first glance, relativism appears persuasive, but a closer look makes us less sure, because no one would accept bizarre local practices—human sacrifices or apartheid, for example. Relativism reduces ethics to nothing more than conducting a proper survey of local customs and laws. The argument to counter relativism is that there are certain universal principles that transcend local custom or practice. These universal principles may be based on fundamental human rights such as life, liberty, and physical well-being. For example, Thomas Donaldson's set of fundamental rights featured in his work *The Ethics of International Business* (1989) is as follows:

- Right to physical movement
- Right to ownership of property
- Right to freedom from torture
- Right to a fair trial
- Right to nondiscriminatory treatment
- Right to physical security
- Right to freedom of speech and association
- Right to minimal education
- Right to political participation
- Right to subsistence

GIVING AWAY YOUR RIGHT OF FREE SPEECH

The third enemy in the workplace is an attitude that prevents challenging ethical egoism (operating for unfair profit and causing harm) and/or ethical relativism (not abiding by universal standards) when they emerge. Not being involved, speaking out, or failing to take action to uphold an ethical standard creates an atmosphere of caution and isolation, which ultimately leads to less productive yield for the energy expended and can cost the company dearly.

Examples of companies with an organizational culture that initially did not actively support verbally challenging the use of ethical egoism and ethical relativism as standards in their planning, decision making, and work practices follow.

In 1985, Martin Marietta Corporation, now Lockheed Martin, the U.S. aerospace and defense contractor, was under investigation for improper travel billings. This event prompted the creation of an internal initiative led by management that resulted in a successful integrity-based program which helped Martin Marietta better compete, fostered a positive workforce morale, and helped establish sustainable relationships with many of their constituencies.

In 1987, the U.S. Food and Drug Administration's investigation of Beech-Nut Nutrition Corporation's misbranding its apple juice led to 10 counts of mislabeling by the courts at an estimated cost of $25 million. Such an error in judgment, to mislead the public for years in believing that Beech-Nut's product contained real apple juice, points to the need for integrity and competence in decision making. Such behaviors do not reflect fair play or business competence. If there is no agreement on standards, the culture will be left to drift in any direction.

In 1988, NovaCare, Inc., then called InSpeech, one of the largest providers of rehabilitation services to hospitals and nursing homes in the United States, lacked a common set of values within the company. It was determined that the result was a 57 percent per year turnover rate. NovaCare created a statement of guidelines for its purpose, fundamental beliefs, and principles. This values initiative led to a reduction in turnover from 57 percent in 1988 to 32 percent in 1990 and a further reduction to 27 percent in 1998. Executives reported that the values statement made a difference; before NovaCare lacked a proactive strategy to promote company integrity.

In 1991, four Salomon Brothers executives failed to take appropriate action when they learned of unlawful activity on the government trading desk. This failure to take action—to respect the standards of trading, the employees, creditors, shareholders, and customers—led to a serious crisis in the confidence in Salomon Brothers' capacity to lead in the investment industry. Salomon Brothers lost nearly $41 billion and severed their bond of trust with the public.

In 1992, Sears, Roebuck and Company received complaints from 40 states about misleading customers by selling unnecessary parts in its vehicle services departments. Although the company's intention was not to defraud customers, its incentive system put undue pressure on salespeople to meet quotas. After a long, drawn-out investigation, the total cost of settlement was estimated at $60 million. This was a clear case where the culture can cause unethical behavior. If the organizational culture has cultivated the standard virtues, the loss of confidence in Sears might have been prevented.

Unfortunately, we have far too many more examples of acting without standard virtues—that is, not Engaging for Good Ends. I often wonder that if we had taken the crises of unethical leadership more seriously in the late 1980s and early 1990s, would there have been the number of scandals we see today—Enron, Worldcom, Tyco, Anderson and Adelphia, to name a few.

There are positive examples, where everyday leaders, choosing free speech in their area of influence, were dramatically displayed in *Time* magazine's Person of the Year issue of December 30, 2002/January 6, 2003, when Cynthia Cooper of Worldcom, Coleen Rowley of the FBI, and Sherron Watkins of Enron adorned the cover representing the virtues in need today around the world. They spoke out and revealed unethical and illegal activities of their organizations. These virtues are the standards of fair play (justice), competence for the good goal (prudence), courage to practice promise keeping (fortitude), and using democratic values to practice self-control when pursuing good ends (temperance) and are embodied in the act of speaking out.

In 1998, Marie Impeggliano and I conducted a critical-incident study identifying ethical and unethical behavior with

200 workers submitting over 600 incidents in 10 different companies in the greater Philadelphia area. From this study, specific patterns showing the need for standards emerged again and again. These areas were as follows: (1) incidents showing a lack of integrity such as failing to uphold and follow up on obvious unethical behaviors (127 incidents) and misleading or not clarifying purpose (22 incidents); (2) incidents showing a lack of productivity such as showing poor judgment in financial decisions (62 incidents); (3) incidents showing a lack of responsibility such as going against company policy and reneging on contracts (17 incidents); (4) incidents showing a lack of respectfulness in relationships such as personally alienating staff (67 incidents) or a lack of professionalism (12 incidents).

Companies can benefit from a strong ethical culture of everyday leaders such as those at Motorola and Johnson & Johnson. Motorola espoused their values to serve as guidelines for action throughout the company. Those values are expressed in simple statements such as, "We will act with uncompromising integrity" and "Hold constant respect for people." Johnson & Johnson's handling of the Tylenol crisis, where packages of Tylenol that were laced with poison were immediately taken off store shelves, was the achievement of many individuals operating from the same values and guiding principles, which reflected the organization's culture.

Such organizational cultures are derived by guidelines that have assisted professionals to act as everyday leaders. The following is an example of a guideline. This accomplishes putting standards for ethical practice in place.

Select the right course of action in planning, decision-making, and business practice on the basis of that which most closely conforms to impartial standards, comprised of the absence of ethical egoism and ethical relativism, to help bring the best overall results for the company and all stakeholders, and to preserve important relations and values in the business profession and with the local community and the society at large.

Adherence to ethics is as important for individuals as it is for organizations. If everyday leaders are prevented from responsibly acknowledging and practicing Engaging for Good Ends, corporate executives run the risk of liability and operating an ineffective and unethical organization. If the organizational system lacks a sense of responsible behavior in its culture, personal choices and decisions on the job will begin to deteriorate into satisfying egoistic needs or taking the easy way out.

Put a good person in an unethical environment and the unethical environment will dominate over the individual. These environments are breeding grounds for egoism and relativism, where good people are infected with the disease. This usually causes ineffectiveness on the job and a lack of discipline in performance.

A good environment encourages everyday leadership. Everyday leaders who embody exemplary ethics stimulate an active effort for more disciplined and effective performance by all stakeholders, not just working to satisfy legal compliance. This will lead to more than just the reduction of business misconduct. It will lead to a more successfully run organization.

In his work, *A Credo for Performance Technologists*, Odin Westgaard explains the need to use our individual sphere of influence in a way that allows us to Engage for Good Ends:

> The basic value which identifies true professionals is their drive to give full measure and do their best. To do less, to settle for a half-measure, is disrespectful of oneself, others, and a profession. Failure to establish ethical controls results in unfair competition, misunderstandings with clients and risks of scandals to the profession. Any professional must seek to lessen the possibility of unfair competition practices by establishing and adhering to ethical guidelines (Westgaard, 1988).

EVERYDAY LEADERS ACTING WITH ETHICAL STANDARDS HELP CREATE AN ETHICAL CLIMATE

Besides Westgaard's reasons for expanding ethical awareness, there is another equally compelling reason. Only by being aware of ethical considerations themselves can everyday leaders help others Engage for Good Ends in their sphere of influence. Every-

day leaders can help their organizations recognize that the ethical climate is one of the environmental factors that affect performance and productivity. For instance, the motivation of
members in a work system can be negatively influenced by:

- Inconsistent application of policies
- Lack of concern for the rights or safety of the individual
- Failure of the organization to comply with the law
- Misrepresentation to suppliers or clients

Likewise, withholding information or establishing unrealistic expectations in an attempt to gain control or to wield
power is an unethical act that damages performance output.
This becomes even more damaging if the fear to voice concerns about unfairness or abuse of power outweighs the desire
to speak. Choosing not to speak out restricts the rights of people in a work system, which can have a major negative impact
on the results of the work process. Operating from the premise
that creating and maintaining an ethical environment ought to
be within the mission of an effective organization (as well as
being a good business practice), everyday leaders should be
able to address ethical concerns in a straightforward manner
without the fear of banishment or punishing sanctions. Members should be able to suggest— without the fear of reprisal—
the need to examine the ethical congruence of the different
functions, policies, and levels of the organization to assure an
environment that encourages exemplary performance.

A solution implemented at one level will have an ethical
impact on the organization as a whole. This systemic approach
to Engaging for Good Ends heightens members' awareness
that a policy established to solve an ethical concern at one level
may cause more concerns or problems elsewhere. To think sys-
temically is one of our ethical responsibilities.

PURPOSE OF STANDARD VIRTUES

The purpose of standard virtues such as integrity, productivity, and responsibility is to serve as a general set of ethical

guidelines for use by everyday leaders. (Another virtue, temperance and the practice of self-control, is dealt with in the next interpersonal skill of the L.E.A.D.E.R.S. Method, Respond with Respectfulness, which is discussed later in the book.) Everyday leaders can become the standard bearers for leadership virtues in any system in which they serve.

These standard virtues were derived from standards on ethics from seven different professional organizations (American Psychological Association, Society of Human Resource Management, American Management Association, American Educational Research Association, American Evaluation Association, Academy of Human Resource Development (AHRD), and the Human Systems Development Group). I was one of six on the team that developed the Standards on Ethics and Integrity for AHRD.

These standard virtues are for everyday leaders to use as they practice the interpersonal skill of Engaging for Good Ends. The standard virtues are not comprehensive, but they do serve as a good start for the everyday leader, and there is space for interpretation and application.

STANDARD VIRTUES FOR THE EVERYDAY LEADER

Anyone can adopt these traits when leading in their own sphere of influence.

1. Integrity (fair play with a sense of justice)
2. Productivity (prudent competence at work to achieve good goals)
3. Responsibility (the fortitude to practice courage when keeping promises and overcome fear)

The form and forces of global change have created a greater need for these standard virtues. The forms of change are manifest in sociopolitical, economic, competitive, customer satisfaction, and technological realms. The forces within these forms include cost effectiveness; a reduction in the amount of time to communicate, manufacture, deliver, and respond; customized service; an emphasis on product quality;

technological advancements; creation of learning organizations to deal with product life cycles; and knowing customers
better than they know themselves. The standard virtues are
described in the paragraphs following.

FAIR PLAY MEANS JUSTICE AND INTEGRITY AT WORK

In *An Inquiry into the Nature and Causes of the Wealth of
Nations*, Adam Smith (1776) writes that everyone, as long as
he does not violate the laws of justice, is free to pursue his
own interest and to bring that interest into competition with
anyone. This is a description of fair play, not an excuse for
foul play.

Hold to this advice and live by it to a fault, using the law as
the only standard. I believe they misconstrue Adam Smith's
premise for their own egoistic agendas. What they may not
know is that Adam Smith also wrote the "Theory of Moral
Sentiment" 17 years earlier than his first-cited treatise. In this
earlier publication (which appeared in his *Essays Philosophical
and Literary*, 1759) about the ethics involved in commerce, he
clearly indicates that however selfish a person can be, there
are some principles in his nature that make him interested in
the fortune of others and their happiness as well. Smith
remarks that this interest in others involves "fair play" and
that without an ethical foundation, the fabric of human society
would crumble.

Ethical egoism is simply not viable in professional business, especially when the health, protection, and welfare for
all stakeholders are concerns. If it is defined as the right to
maximize self-interest and comply only with the law, with little regard for any other standard when dealing with people in
business, ethical egoism must be rejected. It would seem
Adam Smith cared about people as much as he cared about
the need for fair play in business. Fair play imbues business
arrangements with integrity; it is one of the core needs in business. Without fair play there is no connection between people's efforts to succeed and their access to opportunities to
develop optimal talents and be productive for the betterment
of society. Everyday leaders who practice the standard virtue

of integrity—fair play with a sense of justice—exhibit the characteristics described below.

Characteristics of Integrity and Justice
Everyday leaders have integrity. They are honest, play fair, and act in good faith in all dealings with others in the company. They are aware of their own belief systems, values, needs, and limitations; recognize how they might differ from those of others; and are conscious of the potential effect of these differences on their work. They refrain from making false, misleading, or deceptive statements, and they strive always to provide accurate information. They avoid conflict-of-interest relationships, expensive gift giving, bribery, and abuse of government relationships. They clarify to all parties the exact nature of their performance and function. They act with the expectation that each business exchange is one of many more to come—that is, they act with the intention of establishing a long-term business relationship.

PRUDENT COMPETENCE AT WORK
Productivity, competence, and prudence are inextricably linked. Productivity results from competence, which results from a prudent approach where proper goals are aimed for and intelligence is used to achieve them.

Productivity relies on exemplary performance by workers. Individual performance can become exemplary if the organizational culture espouses the standard virtues cited above. The mechanics to improve performance and productivity within an ethical culture demand a mutually reinforcing organizational situation.

Too often merely average performance in a group is acceptable, and that leads to a complacent culture. Once employee complacency sets in, it begins to deteriorate performance, especially if there is no ethical foundation. When that slip in performance begins, individuals in organizations are increasingly resistant to efforts to bring about improvement of good ends and good performance in the culture. Performance and productivity can be improved—and stay improved—if the organization and its employees share the same standard virtues.

Characteristics of Prudence, Competency, and Productivity
Everyday leaders are expected to be knowledgeable about all aspects of their profession and to perform their work in an exemplary fashion. They exercise careful judgment to protect those for whom they are responsible. They use appropriate information, resources, incentives, research, and applications to secure the best service for each stakeholder. They are aware of cultural, individual, and role differences involving age, gender, race, ethnicity, national origin, religion, sexual orientation, disability, language, and socioeconomic status. They work continually to eliminate the effect of biases on work in the company. They do not condone or participate in unfair or discriminatory practices of any kind. They strive to advance individual and organizational learning, performance, and development while mitigating the causes that prevent stakeholder welfare. They comply with laws and social policies that serve the interests of stakeholders, the public, society, and the environment. They have the ability to:

- Establish and manage client relationships
- Conduct analyses
- Identify root causes of conflicts
- Build partnerships within the firm
- Negotiate
- Resolve conflict
- Embrace technology
- Build consensus and commitment
- Manage projects
- Communicate well
- Facilitate the leadership, implementation, and management of change

TAKING RESPONSIBILITY FOR FORTITUDE AND PROMISE KEEPING

Promise keeping is a core need in business. It's not just the right thing to do; it is critical for the stability of business transactions. Although there have been some well-publicized scandals to the contrary, for most traders at the New York Stock Exchange their word is their bond. Without this standard virtue, a promise on Wall Street is of no value. If you choose to be flexible about promise-keeping on Wall Street, you severely limit your chances of success—if you are not black-balled altogether. There are other business promises that are no less important: Professionals have a tacit responsibility not to bring harm to another individual, department, company, community, or society.

Characteristics of Responsibility, Fortitude, and Promise-Keeping

Everyday leaders uphold the law, practice ethical standards, and prevent harm to any stakeholder. They consult with colleagues and clients regarding the ethical compliance in their professional duties. They engage in proper business conduct to prevent unethical dilemmas. They share credit for work accomplishments, when appropriate, and they are trustworthy. They serve the company by honoring all contracts, promises, and commitments. Moreover, they fulfill their professional responsibilities to the community in which they work and live, to the society in which they belong, and to sustaining a livable planet. They understand that there is a necessary confluence of a healthy ecosystem, government, economy, and organizations.

SPECIFIC PRACTICES OF THE EVERYDAY LEADER ENGAGING FOR GOOD ENDS

Summarized on the next page are specific practices of the everyday leader who is Engaging for Good Ends.

- Integrity and justice
  - Uphold honesty, fair play, and good faith actions.
  - Refrain from false, misleading, and deceptive statements.
  - Avoid conflict-of-interest relationships.
  - Disclose and clarify the intentions of all policies, procedures, and processes.
- Prudence, competence, and productivity
  - Know all aspects in your area of responsibility.
  - Exercise careful judgment in the use of your expertise.
  - Know the mechanics to create a productive environment.
  - Master communication, management, and leadership skills.
  - Work toward advancement of a bias-free, work environment.
  - Strive for continual learning of skills and broadening of knowledge.
- Fortitude and responsibility
  - Uphold the standard virtues in application to free enterprise.
  - Comply with your assigned duties and proper business conduct.
  - Honor all promises, commitments, and contracts.
  - Cause no harm.
  - Be aware of your responsibility to the community and society.

TWO OTHER CONSIDERATIONS WHEN ENGAGING FOR GOOD ENDS

Normative theories for Engaging for Good Ends have been suggested for centuries, beginning with the pre-Socratics in the sixth century B.C. There are three considerations regarding performance. We have already discussed the first consideration above, that is, Aristotle's concept of intentionality as described for the everyday leader as the standard virtues.

The other two basic considerations are Kant's universal rules for performance and Bentham and Mill's perspective on the consequences or results of performance. Each of these considerations represents a different vantage point regarding decision making for the everyday leader.

UNIVERSAL RULES

Whereas the consequentialist conducts an analysis in determining alternatives to Engaging for Good Ends, the universal rule is more concerned with a means evaluation. What matters here is the nature of the act in question, not just its results. This is based on a set of rules.

Rules-based practices "attempt to generate a total set of expectations that seem to preserve important relations and values" (Brady, 1990, p. 22). Many ethical theories have been developed from this perspective; the most prominent is reason-based ethics as explained by Kant.

Immanuel Kant pursued principles for Engaging for Good Ends that do not rest on consequences but define actions as inherently right or wrong, apart from circumstantial factors. Kant believed that rules for Engaging for Good Ends were a result of reason alone and that reason guided the beliefs. His idea of pure reason recognized the "possibility of discovering and knowing moral laws or principles without necessarily liking them or experiencing them, but just by recognizing their authenticity" (Brady, 1990, p. 49). For example, telling the truth inherently possesses ethical worth.

Kant's theory, called the Categorical Imperative, is composed of three basic rules:

1. *The Principle of Universality.* An action is morally right for a person in a certain situation if and only if the person's reason for carrying out the action is a reason that he or she would be willing to have every person act on, in any similar situation. In other words, if you are applying the principle of universality, you must be willing to have your action become a universal law for others to

follow in similar situations. One rule of thumb is to ask yourself, "Would I feel comfortable discussing this action on *60 Minutes* or in front of my grandmother?"

2. *The Principle of Reversibility.* The person's reasons for acting must be reasons that he or she would be willing to have all others use, even as a basis of how they treat him or her. This golden rule of Engaging for Good Ends requires that in assessing an action, you ask yourself: "How would I like it if I were treated this way?" If you would wish the same action on yourself, then it meets the requirements of the reversibility principle.

3. *The Principle of Respect for Persons.* "Rational creatures should always treat other rational creatures as ends in themselves and never as only a means to an end" (Shaw and Berry, p. 64). To meet this requirement, a person must do two things: (1) Respect the freedom of others by treating them only as they have consented to be treated. (2) Develop each person's capacity to choose freely among alternatives.

It was Kant's contention that all human beings possess inherent worth and should be treated with the moral dignity to which they are entitled. (This principle is described in detail in Chapter 8, Respond with Respectfulness.)

Balance is the key word in understanding Kant's use of rules. When consistency is lacking as rules are applied, it creates an unfair playing ground. This can result in a lack of balance between morals and values. As a consequence, individuals are disinclined to perform by the rules. They may be less productive, and unethical behavior may become easier to justify. Also, an overemphasis on justice as discussed earlier can reduce entrepreneurship, innovation, and productivity.

CONSEQUENCES AND RESULTS (UTILITARIANISM)

Consequentialism examines the net benefit produced for all stakeholders, primarily the stakeholders who hold stock in a company. It evaluates an action in terms of the efficiency and effectiveness of its consequence. Thus, the rightness or wrongness of an action is determined by its consequences. People's rights, duty, sense of justice, and values are not of primary consideration, just the consequences. "The end justifies the means" is one of the expressions used to describe consequentialism. As mentioned above, ethical egoism and ethical relativism can impair judgment as it concerns Engaging for Good Ends.

Consequentialism suggests that planning, calculating, decision making, and evaluation can encourage creativity, innovation, productivity, and entrepreneurship. Consequentialism should result in the best possible consequences for the organization's goals. These consequences maximize the satisfaction of the organization's constituencies, usually the owners. One question that a consequentialist asks is, "Which action will produce the greatest good?" To answer this question, he or she also must ask which action produces the greatest good for whom. In answering the latter half of this question, the field of consequentialism can be explained as utilitarianism.

Utilitarianism examines consequences to others. Business is comfortable with utilitarian theory because it traces its roots to Adam Smith, the father of modern economics. Yet, as we discussed earlier, Adam Smith wrote about utilitarianism and he wrote persuasively about duty and justice. Utilitarian theory was further defined by the research of Jeremy Bentham (repr. 1979) and John Stuart Mill (repr. 1957). These two men used utilitarian standards to evaluate and criticize the social and political systems of their time period. As a result, utilitarianism is commonly associated with social improvement.

There are a variety of factors, in addition to social improvement and avoiding harm that make utilitarianism attractive in today's world. Some factors are that it:

- Provides a basis for formulating and testing policies.
- Provides an objective way to resolve conflicts of self-interest.
- Recognizes the four primary stakeholders: owners, employees, customers, and society.

- Provides the latitude in moral decision making that organizations seem to need.

Bentham is well known for his "greatest happiness" principle. His concept of the greatest good for the greatest number of people is based on the outcome that produces the most happiness for all persons. The reason Bentham was so interested in this principle is that it provided the rationale for advocating reform of laws and institutions that protected only the traditionally preferred classes of citizens, while dealing harshly with others. Tradition, he felt, often discriminated, but the greatest happiness principle did not; it gave equal weight to every individual.

An additional appeal of utilitarianism is its emphasis on efficiency. "Efficiency is a means to higher profits and to lower prices, and the struggle to be maximally profitable seeks to obtain maximum production from limited economic resources" (Beauchamp and Bowie, 1988, p. 26).

Examples of utilitarianism in today's business and industry are shown below. Each of these activities determines the worth of a situation by evaluating the consequences for all persons affected by the action.

- Cost-benefit analysis
- Environmental impact studies
- The majority vote
- Product comparisons for consumer information
- Tax laws
- Consumer behavior in the free market

From the overall perspective of consequentialism, it becomes easy to overlook the means (the behavior) used to achieve the actual ends (the accomplishment). In addition, the long-term consequences are often not taken into account. In his work, *The Cost of Talent*, Derek Bok suggests that decision makers should periodically assess managerial strategies to be sure that all of the organization's constituencies are being considered, not just the compensation packages for executives.

These three vantage points (standard virtues, universal rules, and utilitarian consequences) involve everyday leaders' continually examining their own sense of right and wrong and revising it as appropriate. With just a basic understanding of each vantage point, everyday leaders can help expand their awareness of the importance of Engaging for Good Ends.

ENGAGING FOR GOOD ENDS IS IMPORTANT. NOW WHAT?

Everyday leaders can activate the standard virtues, the universal rules, and the utilitarian consequences in every conversation and give direction for rethinking organizational culture. An everyday leader can be the standard bearer for such an organization. The question remains: How to go about it.

Everyday leaders should be concerned with any situation in which there is an actual or potential harm to an individual or group at any and all levels of the organization. The harm may be physical, mental, or economic. It is also a concern when the rights of one individual compete with the rights of another or when rights of different levels of the organization compete with each other. Cooke focuses on these situations by raising several questions:

- Is the behavior or anticipated behavior arbitrary or capricious? Does it unfairly single out any individual or group?
- Does the behavior or anticipated behavior violate moral and legal rights of any individual or group?
- Does the behavior or anticipated behavior conform to accepted ethical/moral standards?
- Are there alternative courses of action that are less likely to cause harm?

Such questions should be raised whenever there is actual or potential harm. Patricia McLagan (1997) indicates that all professionals (I would add everyday leaders) should be aware of the following key ethical issues.

- Confidentiality
- Inappropriate requests

- Intellectual property
- Truth in claims
- Organizational versus individual needs
- Customer and user participation
- Conflicts of interest
- Personal biases
- Individual and population differences
- Appropriate interventions
- Intervention consequences
- Fair pricing
- Usage of power

Administrators typically look at the financial data collected, transform it into information to be used in decision making, and judge the consequences of using that information. This approach often leads to an ends-justifies-the-means logic that may fail to provide a complete ethical climate. This logic is utilitarian, or goal-oriented management. But there are two other considerations, as we discussed above. The everyday leader can practice all three.

Organizational issues that present opportunities for everyday leaders to practice ethics to Engage for Good Ends include:

- Employee rights: due process, privacy
- Sexual harassment
- Whistle blowing
- Misuse of power
- Intrinsic motivation
- Selection and placement
- Corporate culture
- Corporate social responsibility
- Agreed-upon incentive system vs. actual system
- Terminations
- Organizational structure, design, and politics
- Performance appraisals

- Drug testing, physical exams
- Diversity discrimination
- Planning, policy, control
- Government relations
- Safety health issues
- Technical development
- Foreign payments
- Environment protection
- Product safety, reliability
- Quality management
- Purchasing (gifts, bribes)
- Automation, robotics

Everyday leaders must address these issues one conversation at a time, and everyone is responsible for exercising caution regarding these issues.

ETHICS TRAINING

A survey of organizations indicates that the following materials and formats are most commonly used in ethics training:

- Codes of ethics (79%)
- Lectures (63%)
- Workshops and seminars (53%)
- Case studies (46%)
- Films and discussion (41%)

Case studies and discussions have been found most effective. "They give participants a sense of how to analyze and resolve ethical problems in a way that is consistent with the company's code or standards of corporate conduct" (Berenbeim, 1987).

Everyday leaders are uniquely positioned in their systems to facilitate the awareness of Engaging for Good Ends. The actual process of making ethical decisions is seldom as easy as simply selecting the correct alternative. Although everyday leaders will sometimes face obvious choices between right and wrong, there usually will be extenuating circumstances. Sometimes the choice will be between one right and another right. These are the tough decisions. With such choices, it is helpful to apply a step-by-step decision-making process. When confronted with choosing between two "right" alternatives, ethical decisions depend on both the decision-making process and the experience, intelligence, and integrity of the decision maker. Sometimes, training and coaching can enhance the decision-making process and enrich the experience of the decision maker. Most decision making relies on P. H. Werhane's seven-step process for ethical decision making (Werhane),which is summarized as follows:

1. *Identify the relevant facts.* Identify key factors that shape the situation and influence Engaging for Good Ends.
2. *Define the issues.* Identify all issues related to the situation and separate the ethical issues from the nonethical issues. Issues may be identified at all levels of the organization.
3. *Identify the primary stakeholders.* Individuals and groups who will be affected by a decision are the primary stakeholders. The impact of a decision on them must be considered.
4. *Determine the possible alternatives.* All alternative interventions need to be identified.
5. *List the implications of each of the alternatives.* Evaluate each alternative according to the impact on the stakeholders and the three considerations discussed above.
6. *List the practical constraints.* Identify any factors that might limit the implementation of alternatives or render it too difficult or risky.
7. *Determine which actions should be taken.* After weighing the information provided in steps 1 through 6, select an alternative and an implementation strategy.

RESPOND WITH RESPECTFULNESS

Carl Rogers would have referred to respectfulness as the natural, internal mechanism where you value your own urge to strive for unconditional positive regard to another person. You would be accepting and prizing the other person in the conversation, thus creating a nonjudgmental and nonevaluative atmosphere where both persons value themselves and the conversation. Rogers referred to this as a person-centered approach to communication where interpersonal qualities help a person lead in a nonauthoritarian way. In their 1939 *Journal of Social Psychology* article, "Patterns of Aggressive Behavior in Experimentally Created Social Climates," Kurt Lewin, Ron Lippitt, and Ralph White demonstrated how nonauthoritarian leadership is effective in consistently increasing the productivity of members at work. These members cooperated and demonstrated more initiative than other groups as a result of the democratic leadership conditions. Aggressive and possibly abusive behavior was reduced because of these conditions.

Peter Block (1996) refers to these characteristics as authentic behavior where the words reflect the actual experience of the communication at that moment in time. It is important to understand that the everyday leader is not "doing something" to the other person. He or she is simply relying on the basic capacity of natural human leadership to develop themselves in an arena of honest expression, creative discussion, and responsibility.

This person-centered, nonauthoritarian arena can be created one conversation at a time. Given the amount of aggression and emotional abuse being expressed in the corporate, public, and government settings today, this practice is of great worth for everyday leaders. Also, it is with this practice, I believe, that one can reduce and dismantle the nature of separatism in our society, one conversation at a time. It helps to create a climate of openness, integrity, productivity, and honesty.

Respect toward individuals and relationships combines such values as accountability, equality, patience, freedom, truthfulness, human rights, and liberty. We can't have human rights without accepting our responsibilities and duties to each other in society. Both rights and duties arise in relationships. Freedom is a right to dignity; a successful response to duty is measured in contributions to others, the company, the community, and society.

Understanding the differences in our dialogues and willingly confronting those differences with the long term in mind, builds trust; and it is impossible to build trust without treating people with respect and dignity. Aggressive and passive aggressive behavior toward another person can destroy interpersonal relationships. Assertive behavior, on the other hand, if it is delivered in a nonthreatening way, can build trust. Assertive behavior requires focus on the task and the people completing the task, and it demands respect to people's rights in conversations. This is honest behavior, which can enhance credibility as it helps you practice courage.

RESPECTFULNESS IN RELATIONSHIPS

Because everyday leaders recognize the value of respect, they are concerned about the intrinsic worth of individuals and their interactions with each other. They also are concerned about their rights to privacy, confidentiality, and self-direction. Everyday leaders advocate against managers' restricting individuals' rights at work. They are aware of the potential conflict between certain legal obligations such as compliance policies and procedures, and the exercise of individual rights. When conflict does occur among stakeholders' obligations, concerns, and rights, everyday leaders attempt to resolve these conflicts responsibly and ethically avoiding, or at least, minimizing harm to others. They are sensitive to power differences among all stakeholders and do not mislead or exploit other people. Respectfulness in relationships creates confidence among stakeholders.

Everyday leaders who Respond with Respectfulness in relationships follow these practices:

- Honor the intrinsic worth and dignity of all individuals.
- Honor the liberty, human rights, and freedom of all individuals.
- Be sensitive to power differences that threaten freedom.
- Be aware of potential conflict between rights and duties.
- Resolve all conflicts with honesty and patience, not coercion.
- Create a good reputation for dependability and responsiveness.
- Avoid fear of speaking about these standards with others.
- Practice courage in upholding these standards.

You are a member of the global economy, who has a potential contribution to make to the workplace, to your family, and to the society at large. Each time you take action using these skills, you contribute. Respect for each individual and every relationship along the way has a connection with how well we do. People usually don't respect oppression or coercion. Respect each person. For respect between individuals to be more prevalent regardless of the group to which they belong requires a reduction and an eventual elimination of prejudice in the workplace.

HOW PREJUDICE RELATES TO RESPECT

Prejudice is an attitude of readiness to respond in a favorable or unfavorable manner to a particular person without sufficient warrant. This attitude includes concepts, feelings, and behaviors. The conceptual level may be the result of an unclear perception of reality. The feeling level varies from positive to negative. The behavioral level manifests in action where a person "talks about them," "avoids them," "denies access," or "speaks out" in acts of discrimination. There are many ways to reduce discrimination through legal and economic means, but it is harder to reduce prejudice on the conceptual and feeling level. But, it is possible if we Respond with Respectfulness one conversation at a time. Practicing respect increases the potential for more and more respect to be present in the workplace.

The effects of discrimination on a person include lowered self-esteem, self-hatred, and negative self-image culminating in a sense of inferiority. Additionally, the effects lead to a willingness to fail where the person avoids the possibility of success in competition because of an expected negative reaction to their success.

The roots of prejudice usually are born by early socialization, parental modeling, the information media, and punishments in life. Prejudice is maintained in the fabric of society by social support where one is guaranteed access to a social group if one agrees with the prejudice. Another way prejudice is maintained is by the number of times the prejudice is evoked so as to recall it to mind many times. However, the major factor in maintaining prejudice to the point where it becomes resistant to change, is in the use of stereotypes. Stereotypes are concepts and perceptions shared by a given group without question, which overemphasize group differences, distort reality, and justify hostility. Stereotypes involve judgments about mannerisms, beliefs, values, and traits of others.

Gordon Allport (1954) suggests that stereotyping enables individuals to manage information efficiently. Information must be categorized in order to handle details. Individuals oversimplify their experience by selectively attending to certain categories and generalizations. These categories are often false generalizations. As people become more aware of the mental structures they have created to store information and the false generalizations that have resulted, the door is open to possible change. In their 1999 article "Confronting Prejudice and Stereotypes: A Teaching Model," Annie McKee and Susan Schor contend that the first steps in dealing with prejudice and stereotypes is to get the facts. Facts provide food for thought and pave the groundwork for change.

Another component of dealing with prejudice and stereotypes is to be aware of oneself as both a target and perpetrator of prejudice and stereotypes. Individuals may not be aware of higher-order thought processes which allow them to make inaccurate assessments of others, behave accordingly, and simply not realize it. McKee and Schor propose that self-awareness enhances people's motivation to change attitudes and behaviors and increase the feeling of personal responsibility toward others as well as a willingness to help others. Moreover, change in attitude and behavior can result from the cognitive dissonance experienced by individuals when they become aware that their prejudice is in conflict with their own values and self-image.

As we discussed earlier in the book, empathy as a communications tool results in shaping positive behavior and enabling a more accurate and complete understanding of others' actions and reactions. Empathy also is a major factor in encouraging pro-social behavior; McKee and Schor believe that factual information, self-awareness, and empathy can help people to better understand the source of differences and as such aid in dismantling prejudice and stereotyping.

Everyday acts of leadership that reduce prejudice might include:

•   Speak in conversations to increase the ethical and social contact among alien groups

•   Respond in conversations to create a climate of equality of status and equal participation toward a common goal

•   Be vigilant in all forms of communication to increase the positive attitude toward interracial contact

•   Practice consciousness-raising techniques in any and all conversations

---

CASE STUDY OF EVERYDAY LEADERSHIP
FROM A SENIOR WOMAN AT VERIZON

As a new leader in the corporate world, I thought I knew all about the proper way to respond to any given situation or person. My high school and college years were replete with opportunities to accept or pursue leadership roles. Whether it was as the President of my college chapter of the National Student Association or the leader of my college sorority, I thought I had been exposed to challenges and opportunities that had shaped my ability to be respectful at all times in any given situation. I had been fortunate to lead other people like me who were focused on clear-cut common goals and could learn what was needed to get the job done. Why should it be different once I left the halls of learning and entered the boardrooms of corporate America?

My first lesson in reality and the importance of responding with respect came within the first three months of my now 26-year career in business. It remains etched in my conscious and subconscious memory. I refer to it often, when it is appropriate, during mentoring sessions, to remind those I am mentoring of the importance of a respectful response, particularly in times of frustration.

I was a "fresh out of college, assistant manager in the Operator Services division in a western Pennsylvania city, charged with the responsibility of training and developing 27 long-distance operators, most of whom had worked for the company for far more years than I had been alive. The senior operator who was assigned to support me was my chief assistant as we struggled to exceed objectives such as average work time, average time to answer an incoming customer call, and courteous and professional treatment of

our customers. Our results, as measured by several performance indicators, were impressive. Our trend lines demonstrated improvement and morale on our team was fairly
healthy despite the grueling job requirements.

One day, my manager asked to see me in her office and
told me that a new operator would be joining my team. I
silently groaned when I thought of a lengthy learning curve
and time my senior operator and I would have to invest to
"break her in." I was relieved, however, when my manager
explained that my new operator had many years of prior
experience as an operator, albeit on older technology, and was
merely reentering the workforce after an absence during
which she raised her children.

My concerns were allayed, but once I met my new operator and observed her during her first week of training, I
knew I had my hands full. She was unable to accomplish
what I thought were the simplest tasks associated with being
a long-distance operator. I had to repeat portions of lessons
many times for it to "sink in," and often I was not really sure
if it indeed was sinking in at all. My level of frustration was
mounting.

It reached its crescendo when I took her from the safe
environment of the training room to a live operator position
with incoming calls from real customers. I sat alongside her
for some time, and then left her to work alone when I
thought she was capable of working without close supervision. But, she called on me repeatedly for assistance. After
countless calls from her, I briskly walked from my desk to
her operator position and in full view and ear-shot of other
operators, responded somewhat curtly with, "And what do
you want now!?" Needless to say, I didn't respond with
respect.

There were inaudible gasps from other operators. I had
not noticed it when I approached her position, but she was
already on the verge of tears. I immediately closed her position to prevent more customer calls from coming in and told
her to accompany me to a nearby conference room where we

could meet privately. Many tissues later, she explained the obvious—that she knew she was in over her head and that she felt powerless to do anything about it. After a much-needed apology from me for my lack of sensitivity and respect, we made a pact to work together to attempt to make her a productive operator and contributing employee. I also apologized to the other operators who had observed my exchange with her for the lack of respect I had given her.

The happy ending was that though she never achieved outstanding levels of productivity, she improved enough to become a contributing member of my team. And I learned a valuable lesson about the importance of a respectful response no matter how frustrating the person or circumstances may be.

In an article written for *The Financial Times* in October 2001, "Upholding Standards for Ethical Practice" by Peter Dean, it was explained that professionals recognize, respect, and are concerned about the worth of individuals, their interactions with each other, as well as their rights to privacy and confidentiality within the context of fundamental dignity, financial information, and worth of all people. Respect for the worth and value of individuals is critical if an everyday leader is to successfully achieve his or her team goals. Respect also must extend to the entire organization. Demonstrating that respect often comes in the nature of the tone and frequency of written and spoken communications among everyday leaders as members of the organization. An everyday leader must respond to the needs of the organization, and one of those needs is respectful and frequent communications.

Respect should be evident along with other widely accepted values such as trust, integrity, and forthright communications that course through the veins of all healthy organizations. Leaders should respond to their employees with respect no matter how trying and frustrating the organizational climate might be. As noted previously, demonstrating respect often comes in the form of written and spoken communications that are open, honest, and timely.

Another way everyday leaders demonstrate respect is by modeling behavior that creates a common understanding that they care about individual members of the team as well as the collective team as a whole. James Kouzes and Barry Posner devoted an entire chapter in their 1987 book, *The Leadership Challenge*, to the importance of leaders who demonstrate that they care. Caring leaders, according to Kouzes and Posner, make a difference. Caring leaders respond to their people and their organizations with respect. Kouzes and Posner noted that "leaders enable others to act. They foster collaboration and build spirited teams. They actively involve others. Mutual respect is what sustains extraordinary efforts, so leaders create an atmosphere of trust and human dignity."

It is impossible to respond with respect if you do not care about or are disconnected from the interpersonal aspects of leadership—aspects that develop from having a personal relationship with the team. One might argue that it is impossible to have a personal relationship with an inanimate object such as an organization; that leaders can only have a relationship with individual members of the organization.

However, for one to be as exemplary as an everyday leader, he or she must establish and sustain a personal connection and relationship not only with individual members of the organization, but with the heart and soul of the organization as well. That can only be done with the conscious investment of the everyday leader's time. In spite of numerous priorities that must be juggled simultaneously, the everyday leader must make the conscious choice to invest the time to develop quality interactions and communications on their teams.

If the members of an organization were surveyed, the results could be that everyday leaders are all accessible and regularly engage in straightforward and respectful communications. Once an everyday leader creates that level of rapport within his or her organization and thereby earns a reputation of open communication, responding with respect will flow freely back and forth in both directions, from one everyday leader to other everyday leaders and back again. With respectful communications, organizational goodwill will propagate and the organizational climate will remain strong. Without respectful communications, a company or organization can falter and potentially lose its way.

Such is the case of a company I have the privilege of leading. In the spring of 2002, I was named the president of a non-regulated subsidiary of a large company. In the early years of the company's existence in the mid-1990s, the air was charged with possibility, excitement, and unbridled passion for the certain success that the future held for all who signed on to ride the wave of prosperity. The first employees readily took on the challenge of building their company from scratch. They saw to it that the company was imbued with an entrepreneurial spirit and a "can do" attitude. They were excited about the present and optimistic about the future.

The starting point for them and for all that they hoped to accomplish was rooted in respect for one another and respect for all the challenges and opportunities that lay before them. The company experienced rapid growth in scope of work, geographic reach, and number of employees. Infrastructure requirements in the obvious areas of corporate governance like human resources, finance, operations, sales and marketing, were put into place. There was, however, one notable exception. This exception was a platform based on the leadership team responding with respect to the needs and concerns of the organizational body made up of everyday leaders.

By the time I became its position leader, the company was experiencing severe organizational pains that threatened its very existence. Intradepartmental and interdepartmental teamwork and trust were in need of significant improvement, as evidenced by periodically administered employee satisfaction surveys. Conversations around the proverbial water cooler centered on the invisible wall that had been built over the years between the employees and the leadership team at headquarters. Effective communications had ground to a halt and the entrepreneurial spirit was on life support.

Through a concerted effort by my new leadership team and me, we identified the root cause as failed communications and began to systematically close the gap between employees and their leaders. An everyday leader council made up of representatives from every department in the company was formed. Based on feedback from surveys, attention was given to key drivers of employee satisfaction. Two of those drivers were the employees feeling valued and open and honest communications in the company. Though the everyday leadership team did not realize it at the time, we were embarking on a transformational experience on the value of responding with respect to the needs of the members and the company.

Members had told us in very stark terms that they not only wanted to be valued, respected, and heard, but that they demanded it. For the everyday leadership team to turn a deaf ear on these demands would have meant certain peril to the future of the company, particularly since its value to the parent company was being scrutinized and challenged from time to time. A communications coach who had formerly focused on external communications was directed to refocus on internal communications. It had become apparent that communications from the everyday leadership team to the other members needed to be proactive but also from the tone that everybody was an everyday leader. Department heads began holding regularly scheduled open dialogue sessions and the everyday leadership team became extremely visible throughout the entire company. The increased accessibility of the everyday leadership team was evidence that more and more members were responding with respect to the needs of the employees and the company. When it became necessary to deliver stressful news to the members, it was done with concern and respect for their feelings and their needs.

The role of the everyday leadership team became invaluable in promoting respectful communications. Team members often screened corporate messages before they were released to ensure that they would be received in the spirit in which they were intended. At all times, respect for the recipients of the intended communication was paramount. Respectful communications could be found not only in formal communications channels, but in informal ones as well. Teamwork began to rebound and morale began to improve.

Over a relatively short period of time, the improvement in the organizational climate was palpable. This was due in large part to the fact that the everyday leadership team learned the valuable lesson in the importance of not only honest communications, but also responding with respect.

The ability to respond with respect cannot be overlooked as a required element in a list of the successful everyday leader's core competencies. An everyday leader must respond with respect in one-on-one situations or in large group settings. An everyday leader must respond with respect in written or verbal communications. And an everyday leader must respond with respect in good times and bad times, times of smooth sailing and times of extreme turbulence. To do so, heightens that person's credibility. Then results like these follow:

- Members are proud to be part of the organization.
- Everyday leaders feel a sense of ownership for the organization.
- There is a sense that everyday leadership is fun.

TO RESPOND TO ANOTHER PERSON

Highly effective everyday leaders seek to understand the nature or origin of the communication and deliver the response in a way that does not alienate or offend. They understand that a respectful response will cultivate improved communications. Genuine communications require respect.

The differences in responsive behavior have fascinated theorists, researchers, and practitioners in the field of psychology for many decades, starting with Sigmund Freud (1917), C. G. Jung (1964), Carl Rogers (1959), Erich Fromm (1941), and Eric Erikson (1959). I know as a learning psychologist, they have fascinated me and I consider myself still teachable in this area. We can divide those differences into four categories (People-focused, Task-focused, Ego-focused, and Image-focused). Understanding these categories of behavioral response in ourselves and in others is useful for the everyday leader. Knowing the best way to respond is showing respect in all conversations.

The four different ways of doing things—that is, the four categories of responding behavior—can all emerge in one individual at different times over the course of a career and a lifetime.

Once we have accepted ourselves as an everyday leader (albeit without a formal title or change in title), it helps to understand how others who work in our sphere of influence perceive us. There are four observable patterns in our behavior, four distinct ways people perceive us. We must consider these four ways if we want to respond fully to another person and if we really care about respecting the dimensions of a person. This skill has the additional benefit that it helps us not to take things personally in our interactions with others.

You will see for yourselves what these observable behaviors accomplish interpersonally. But first, we must see how they began to emerge as classic responses in behavior.

IDEAS OF FREUD, ERIKSON, FROMM, AND ROGERS UNDERPIN FOUR DRIVES IN OUR RESPONSES

The work of Sigmund Freud is always a good starting point from which to understand behavior in relationships. Freud's three psycho-sexual stages or dimensions of character development are:

- *Oral.* People-focused, as in giving support
- *Anal.* Task-focused, as in holding to task perfection
- *Phallic.* Ego-focused, as in taking control

In a sense, drives like these develop our character and personal growth. Wilhelm Reich (1949) defined *character* as an attempt to master the conflicts and impulses we experience as we develop. Character bounds the impulses in a stable way.

Working from Reich's ideas, Fromm and Erikson added a fourth dimension to character development. Fromm spoke of character as either productive or unproductive behavior. Erikson spoke of character development as a general form of functioning in the world.

Fromm talked about healthy human beings being productive at work, Carl Rogers talked about the full functioning personality, and Abraham Maslow talked about self-actualizing people. All wanted to address the obstacles to positively leading everyday in our sphere of influence at work, to relating to others using our individuality, and using our personal power without disallowing others from using theirs. From these ideas, we can begin to make useful some of this knowledge about identifiable patterns of behavior for the everyday leader.

HOW OUR BEHAVIORAL RESPONSE BEGINS IN LIFE

We all start out in life in our own self-concept with whatever endowments and capacities we have received psychologically, emotionally, physically, and intellectually from our parents. All of us began with a capacity to win in life. Each of us has our own unique way of seeing, hearing, thinking, and so on. We all have potentials and limitations. Authenticity in life becomes real by the experience of self with the experience of reality. Almost immediately in living life we begin to try things out to see what works as we grow into the world. Basically, everything we can do can be brought about through four distinct kinds of behavior. These four ways of behaving become part of us with one or two of the behaviors being more frequently used than the other two. Understanding the four modes of behavioral responses allows us to receive information and dialogue that information without taking offense to the way the information is being expressed. The four modes of response are listed here:

1. Care about people with appreciation and sincerity.
2. Care about accuracy and precision in task completion.
3. Care about power, control, and ego gratification while driving for results.
4. Care about image, popularity, and prestige to gain social acceptance.

CARE ABOUT PEOPLE WITH APPRECIATION AND SINCERITY

We begin to get to know *people* and rationally deal with those relationships often making adaptations along the way. One can see this happening with small children at any day care facility or on any playground of a school. With these interactions we learn flexibility, tactfulness, awareness of the needs of others, and what it takes to create and maintain harmony. Some of us are more successful at this than others and we begin to know our natural preferences. The impression others have of this behavior is that people are important.

CARE ABOUT ACCURACY AND PRECISION
IN TASK COMPLETION

As we begin the many thousands of *tasks* and projects that are to be accomplished at work, in school, and at home, we learn how to monitor in a systematic, analytical, and tenacious way. When completing a task, we begin to understand what is reasonable and what may take us off course. We organize around the accomplishment of the tasks and when we interact with someone while in this mode, they get the impression that the task is all-important and you are serious about its completion.

CARE ABOUT POWER, CONTROL, AND EGO GRATIFICATION
WHILE DRIVING FOR RESULTS

From the experience of accomplishing tasks to get results, we learn that the application of *initiating* the energy around a project is necessary as well as being persistent sometimes with a sense of urgency. It is perceiving what needs to be the project to be undertaken and controlling the flow of that project. As we continue in living life, that predisposition turns into a habit of behaving even when initiating energy around an action is not needed. It satisfies the need for ego control but oftentimes leaves the impression that satisfying the ego is more important than the task or the people conducting the task. These impressions more often than not leave a negative feeling of exploitation with the other people experiencing them.

CARE ABOUT IMAGE, POPULARITY, AND PRESTIGE
TO GAIN SOCIAL ACCEPTANCE

We may be helpful and therefore be seen as someone giving ideal support but the real motivator is feeling popular and socially accepted. From this behavior is developed the qualities of advocacy, loyalty, cooperativeness, and principled action as a way of gaining notice and acceptance. While these are laudable qualities, they may leave the impression with others that social acceptance and popularity are more important than the other people involved in the task and the true task at hand.

All four of these kinds of behavioral responses are necessary in interaction. People and Task, which generally emanate from our values, in my opinion, are the most important. I believe we have in the workplace today a system that supports Control and Image, which generally emanates from the political life of the organizational system, more than People and Task. This is evidenced by the overwhelming attention by our society puts on the branding of products and services, oftentimes over inflated. That is untenable if we truly want a workforce that is productive and successful where everyday leadership can be practiced by all members in a work system.

Stuart Atkins (1981) and Drea Zigarmi, Ken Blanchard, Michael O'Connor, and Carl Edeburnn (2005) summed up these four kinds of experiences of human action as:

1. Showing support (people)
2. Conserving-holding (task)
3. Controlling-taking (ego control)
4. Adaptive-dealing (image)

Drawing from the work in this area of many authors and writers, the four kinds of behaviors are discussed below in the context of everyday leadership.

PEOPLE-FOCUSED
Those who are people-focused know people and adapt with tact and flexibility to create or restore harmony. They are caring enablers, helpers at work, and developers of peers or subordinates where they are committed to lofty goals, not the avoidance of work. Douglas McGregor (1960) and Frederick Herzberg (1966) suggested that direction and control are useless in motivating these kinds of behavior and the people that usually use those behaviors and whose important needs are human and social. If these human and social needs are not met there exists indolence, passivity, resistance to change, lack of responsibility, willingness to follow the demagogue, and unreasonable demands for economic benefits. Fred Emery and Einar Thorsdrud (1976) suggest providing for the personal growth and development of members, especially the large numbers at the base of an organization who may feel degraded by their work experiences. Ackoff and Emery (1972) as well as Emery and Emery (1976) suggest using choice in members' decision making by dialogue that communicates to inform and instruct. A message that informs opens up the probability of choice. A message that instructs opens up the perception of probable effectiveness. This leads individuals to want to be more

productive. Robert R. Carkhuff (1984) suggests that people are driven by this productivity value. He states that values are meanings we attach to people and work.

Our earliest basic and living values come from our parents. Carkhuff suggests that the values we develop as adults center around the things and the social experience in the world of work. Thus learning with and from others is an important value in the workplace. When everyday leaders choose to help create an environment at work that supports these notions, he or she may be called an everyday leader in an environment where leadership is not owned by one person but instead floats from person to person as and when necessary.

Acclaimed management thinker Peter Senge (1990) describes this kind of everyday leader as a steward leader. Robert R. Greenleaf (1977) uses the term *servant leader*. I believe both terms are misleading and harness leadership from truly being available to all members in the workplace. The terms may be wrong but not the idea behind the terms. Senge and Greenleaf both agree that this type of behavior should be more availed at work. The behavior practiced by an everyday leader is as caring for the people and the larger purpose or mission of the organization where there is a strong desire to learn. In turn, that mobilizes the forces of the soul beyond a transactional return on equity. I believe an everyday leader is a teacher as well who helps everyone in their sphere of influence to gain greater insight into reality if they can provide that. They are committed to people in their sphere of influence, yet should not make people dependent on them but in fact, offer the opportunity of everyday leadership to other members. People-driven everyday leaders favor peaceful and swift ways of dealing with conflict so that the conflict does not fester.

TASK-FOCUSED

People who are task-focused act in a systematic, analytical way and tenaciously use reason, which actually saves time in the long run. Task-focused everyday leaders are like diplomatic leaders. They are self-reliant, conscientious, create and maintain order, organize operations, and strive to be accurate because they are ruled by strict conscience and have high standards that motivate them to make sure that instructions are followed and costs are kept within the budget lines. They focus on continuous improvement at work, are good team players, and desire to work within their values. They may tend to be a bit narrow and rule-bound in their relationships with others, but when given thorough explanations of a need for change, will change.

Senge (1990) refers to this type of leader as a *designer* who works behind the scenes, planning, fostering strategic thinking, and attempting to govern ideas. I agree. Such leaders like trying to build the foundational policy of an organization out of its purpose and core values. Inner-directed people strive for perfection. These everyday leaders lead in their sphere of influence by expecting others to strive for perfection on their jobs and to obey the rules.

CONTROL-FOCUSED

Control-focused leaders are competent in action and get results by taking control, being persistent, and urgent. Maccoby (2000) does not use this term. Greenberg, Weinstein, and Sweeney (2001) refer to this as ego-driven in relation to self-gratification. I introduce it here, not necessarily as a negative or positive term but as a term that is distinct from the other categories. Using it does fit the framework and can be based on other personality inventories.

This type of leader charges into action. Basically, this leader is independent, innovative, risk-oriented, and driven to achieve for a sense of power and glory. They have expertise and want to be admired, not loved. They act with vision as they see the big picture, but they have no trouble stepping over standards as they aggressively pursue their goals. They may tend into isolation and have a sense of paranoia under stress. They do not listen well at all, easily feel threatened, shun emotions of others, and don't learn in a team very easily, yet their mode of action is reliant on others. They cause a new stimulus to organizational or cultural development but may cause more damage in the long run. They tend to think of themselves as inspirational as they are usually skillful orators but tend to dominate and indoctrinate all the time whenever they speak. Often they need empathy, affirmation, and adulation from others to operate successfully yet they lack the ability to be empathetic and do not like to mentor or be mentored. Many times they are not restrained by a conscience. Ego-driven leaders should get into analysis to learn how to control themselves as they seem more interested in controlling others. It is not common that the ego-driven leader is able to submerge his or her ego for very long, but submerging the ego is necessary to build rapport and support with others. Senge has no category for this type of leader. Ego-driven people need to feel powerful, but they deny other bases of personal power in the workplace and as such, everyday leadership is less practiced unless this kind of behavior is rationed.

IMAGE-FOCUSED

This type of leader strives for excellence with the hope of proving worth and being accepted—principled, cooperative, and dedicated. An image-focused leader needs to feel persuasive and popular. It may stem from a poor self-esteem where the threat of failure is always looming large, but the behavior does have a positive perception and good benefit to others. Erich Fromm talked about this style as a marketing style. Such leaders are less driven by conscience than by the obsessive need to please everyone or serve the populace. The attempt to please everyone is something that comes about because of the anxiety that the image-driven leader creates himself or herself. They have to sell themselves to others to reduce the anxiety of their insecurity. However, using that very drive, they are masters at facilitating teams and keeping the focus on adding value. Thus, they can facilitate everyday leadership as well. They like change and are usually average listeners. They can become exactly like the people they happen to be with in an attempt to satisfy the need to be valued. They do generate enthusiasm and make a favorable impression when contacting people. They will lead when it will bring popularity at which time they may hold on dearly to the leadership opportunity. But, as we have seen, for everyday leadership to exist in a workplace, it has to be allowed to float the person with the best idea, irrespective of rank or popularity.

All of us have within us all four of these character drives. The need to have them be conscious as we choose to change behavior is important. The more we have the ability to choose the kind of behavior we exhibit, the better our own self-concept will be. Some may be more developed than others. Probably, as everyday leaders we need to be able to draw upon all four drives. From others' observation we probably are more of one or two than being all four at once. We probably favor two of the four as a central tendency. Given the situation, all four ways of referral and subsequently doing things are useful at one time or another. However, for everyday leaders the first two drives (people-driven and task-driven) may be most influential. It would seem the corporate world has in the past favored the other two styles (ego-driven and image-driven) for positions of power. I believe the first two character drives can be equally powerful to influence any system of work in a positive, progressive, and productive manner.

Everyday leadership behavior refers to four distinct ways individuals gather and process information due to their personality preferences. Most individuals use two of the four kinds of behaviors primarily.

USING FOUR DIMENSIONS OF EVERYDAY LEADERSHIP

CHARACTERISTICS OF PEOPLE-FOCUSED EVERYDAY LEADERS

- They are socially skillful, flexible, tactful, adaptable, negotiating, animated, inspiring.
- They use a light touch and personal charm to win over people.

- They are flexible in finding ways to satisfy other people.
- They are sensitive to and aware of others' feelings and what will please them.
- They have a sense of humor, which reduces tension.
- They will not blow their own horn or take sole credit, but do appreciate when others recognize their efforts.
- They are diplomatic and careful of people's feelings.
- They are able to see both sides of the argument.
- They are optimistic about outcomes of conflict.
- They may get too involved in socializing and not use time well.
- They become overly entertaining and distract from the seriousness of situations.
- They may lose sight of their own course and not do what is best for those under them, only to feel unappreciated later on.
- They may diffuse seriousness and create an artificial sense of well-being.
- They may be too tactful, and this may cause mistrust about their real thoughts and feelings.
- They may seem to be ambivalent and inconsistent, not standing for anything.
- They are loyal, dependable, team people.
- They are family oriented, with a high degree of trust in long-term relationships.
- They have staying power in relationships once they are committed to people and to the work.
- Their greatest fear is a loss of security.
- They are patient and steady listeners who manifest approachability and warmth.
- Their greatest strength is their patience, steady follow-through, and accommodation, which allows their calm and reassuring behavior to complement their supportive manners.

- Their blind spot is that they are low risk takers, slow to change, and may have difficulty speaking up for themselves, which gives the impression that they agree while inwardly they are not agreeing.

Possible Needs of the People-Focused Everyday Leader
- Security of situation
- Preservation of the status quo unless given reasons to change
- Happy home life
- Traditional procedures for having everyone speak up in a decision-making process
- Sincerity
- Admiration of those who show depth of contribution at work

Tools Needed to Be an Effective People-Focused Everyday Leader
- Preparation before change
- Short-cut methods
- Reassurance of the value and importance of their contributions
- Help in getting started on a new task
- Coworkers with other styles
- Authorization before acting
- Judges others by:
  - Cooperative attitude
  - Loyalty
- Overuses:
  - Indirect approach
  - Tolerance and kindness

Possible Desires of the People-Focused Everyday Leader
- Status quo, steady pace, low-key behavior that results in consistency and follow-through

- Identification with groups
- The opportunity to deal with limited territory
- Security of situation
- Established work patterns
- Acceptance
- Time to adjust
- Areas of specialization

How People-Focused Everyday Leaders Solve Problems
- Observing
- Implementing
- Rigor
- Researching
- Applying
- Reflecting
- Avoiding

Public figures representing this mode of behavior could be Dwight Eisenhower, Walter Cronkite, and Mother Teresa.

CHARACTERISTICS OF TASK-FOCUSED EVERYDAY LEADERS
- They thoroughly examine and study people's needs and situations.
- They follow methods, policies, and procedures to secure details in a cautious and conscientious way.
- They rely heavily on data, analysis, and logic to make decisions.
- They outline tradeoffs.
- They are tenacious with strong opinions.
- They are practical, economical, and tend to look at the whole picture.
- They are reserved.
- They are factual and organized and create order out of chaos.
- They are steadfast.

- They are thorough.
- They are plodding.
- They are nit-picking.
- They are critical.
- They are perfectionists.
- They are sensitive, objective thinkers with intuition, and they make decisions in a logical, cautious way.
- Their greatest fear is criticism of their work as they are comfortable with the use of precision.
- They are accurate and want to know the background of a situation.
- They need many facts or reasons and ask many questions.
- Their blind spot is that they are paralyzed by over-analysis and detail.
- They have difficulty letting go of their conclusions once researched.
- They are uncreative.
- They are stingy.
- They are unfriendly in that they prefer performing tasks to relating with people.
- They confuse people with too many options, preventing action.
- They may not be flexible enough to provide concessions.
- They may not appreciate new ideas.
- They get stuck with old ways when new ones are needed.
- They may appear to be uninvolved because they do not demonstrate their feelings.
- They may withdraw and become distant.
- They may be locked into analysis paralysis.

Possible Needs of the Task-Focused Everyday Leader
- Activities requiring precision
- Ready access to many facts
- Exact job description and objectives

- Less time on details
- Tolerance for conflict
- As much respect for coworkers, as for the work they do
- Judging others by:
  - Thinking ability
  - Logic
- Overuses:
  - Analysis
  - Standard operating procedures

Tools Needed to Be an Effective Task-Focused Everyday Leader
- Security assurance
- Standard way of doing things
- Sheltered environment
- No sudden or abrupt changes
- Opportunities created by others
- Opportunity to be part of a group

Possible Desires of the Task-Focused Everyday Leader
- Security
- Little decision making
- Controlled work environment
- No sudden changes
- Exact job descriptions
- Reassurance
- Personal attention
- Status quo

How Task-Focused Everyday Leaders Solve Problems
- Analyzing
- Investigating
- Evaluating
- Coordinating

- Planning
- Criticizing
- Preferring that things are done the "right way"—according to "the book" or to accepted standards

Public figures representing this mode of behavior could be Katherine Hepburn, Meryl Streep, Jacqueline Kennedy Onassis, and Woodrow Wilson.

CHARACTERISTICS OF CONTROL-FOCUSED EVERYDAY LEADERS

- They show little sensitivity for feelings of others.
- They are control-driven, seek to assume authority, are initiators—like to be in charge.
- They are impatient, always in a time crunch—aggressive.
- Their greatest fear is being taken advantage of, experiencing a loss of control as they become aware that they are falling behind.
- They desires change and like to do many things at once.
- They have a low tolerance for slow learning.
- They must be confronted in a direct, but nonthreatening way.
- Their blind spot is that they move too fast and leave others behind, choosing to get results over developing relationships.
- They may take control when they should not.

Possible Needs of Control-Focused Everyday Leaders

- Difficult assignments
- Becoming aware that they need people
- Basing leadership techniques on practical experience
- Providing explanations of why they do what they do
- Greater awareness of existing sanctions
- Learning to relax more
- Judging others by:
  - Ability to get the task done quickly

- Overuses:
  - Impatience
  - Coolness

Tools Needed to Be an Effective Control-Focused Everyday Leader
- Power and authority
- Prestige
- Accomplishments and results
- Opportunity for advancement
- Wide scope of function
- Freedom from control and supervision
- Many new and varied activities

Possible Desires of the Control-Focused Everyday Leader
- Authority
- Freedom
- "Bottom line" approach
- Opportunity for advancement
- Challenge
- Varied activities
- Correctness
- Prestige
- Growth assignments
- Safety

How Control-Focused Everyday Leaders Solve Problems
- Being pragmatic
- Being efficient—using time to get information without small talk
- Reacting
- Competing
- Deciding
- Domineering

Public figures representing this mode of behavior could include George Patton, Margaret Thatcher, Dan Rather, and Barbara Walters.

CHARACTERISTICS OF IMAGE-FOCUSED EVERYDAY LEADERS

- They guide in their sphere of influence through statements of principles and fairness and optimistic effort.
- They make allowances for people and defend their rights.
- They are overprotective and overly sympathetic with people's interests.
- They may find it difficult to initiate action.
- They are willing to hear other people's positions.
- They are willing to extend themselves to do what is right and fair by others.
- They may rely on others too much when unsure of the situation and may accept unreasonable demands; they also may lack vigilance to the dangers in a situation.
- They may give in rather than be seen as uncooperative.
- They may overidentify with others' objectives instead of their own.
- They become critical of self and others when they can't achieve the impossible.
- They are thoughtful and highly committed to reducing conflict and increasing cooperation.
- They are trusting.
- They are modest.
- They are receptive; willing to hear the other person.
- They are helpful and express interpersonal warmth.
- They are persuasive communicators.
- They are people-oriented and are energized by being with others, regardless of the context.
- Their greatest fears are a loss of approval, lack of inclusion, humiliation, and being unaccepted.
- They are disorganized.
- They are optimists, great encouragers—friendly.

- Their blind spot is that they need to listen more and pay more attention to detail.
- They enjoy talking more than listening.
- They are impatient with being alone.
- They are too focused on others, easily bored, impractical, gullible, obligated, passive, overcommitted, overprotective, and self-deprecating.
- They tend to approach newcomers in an outgoing, gregarious, and socially aggressive manner.
- They tend to be impulsive, emotional, and reactive.

Possible Needs of the Image-Focused Everyday Leader
- More control over time, if low
- Objectivity
- Democratic structure
- Sense of urgency
- Less ideological orientation
- Learning to judge others by:
  - Communication skills
  - Personal contact
- Overuses:
  - Praise
  - Enthusiasm

Tools Needed to Be an Effective Image-Focused Everyday Leader
- Popularity, social recognition
- Public recognition of ability
- Opportunity to talk
- Social activities as part of work
- Democratic relations
- Freedom from control and details

Possible Desires of the Image-Focused Everyday Leader
- Social recognition
- Favorable working conditions

- Chance to motivate people
- Freedom from control and details
- Popularity
- Opportunity to help others
- Freedom of speech
- Availability of people to talk to
- Greater recognition of abilities
- Power

How Image-Focused Everyday Leaders Solve Problems
- Supporting
- Experimenting
- Trusting
- Appearing
- Using instinct
- Depending on others

Public figures representing this mode of behavior could be Will Rogers, Carol Burnett, Liza Minelli, and Bill Cosby.

These four kinds of behavior are perceived by others as our response to them and their work. It is important to understand that is what is being perceived. Within these four categories of responses, one element must be common. That element is respect. Oddly enough, from my experience, people-driven and task-driven kinds of behavior engender slightly more respect from others than ego-driven and image-driven kinds of behavior.

The term *respect* is given attention in rhetoric of the workplace. In order to have the value of respect readily available however, it is necessary to understand that one can be respectful using each of the four kinds of behavior but may want to give a healthy blend of all four in their everyday leadership repertoire. Secondly, there is a deeper understanding about the notion of respect than is commonly understood.

9

SPEAK WITH SPECIFICITY

Speaking with Specificity is the last interpersonal skill in the L.E.A.D.E.R.S. Method. Assuming that we have received and comprehended all parts of a message, do we send messages that others can comprehend? Is our message aligned verbally, vocally, and visually with our intent? Speaking is conveying specifically our actual intent and knowledge to someone else.

In his seminal work, *What Communication Means*, Peter Drucker (1974) recollected a key insight about the skill, Speaking with Specificity, with reference to a remark Mary Parker Follett made in the 1930s. She suggested that disagreement or conflict is likely not to be about the answer. In many cases, the conflict results from incongruity in communication between two people. What "A" sees so vividly, "B" does not see at all; and, therefore, what "A" argues is not pertinent to "B's" concerns and vice versa. Both see different aspects of the same reality, so there is no possibility of true communication.

Follett's remark strikes at the very heart of the importance and the difficulty of speaking with shared meaning, giving rise to the need for Speaking with Specificity. Even if the three basic elements (verbal, vocal, and visual) of a message are defined and designed to optimize the transfer from the sender, the receiver of the message needs to be listening actively to receive the message as mentioned before. It is appropriate that the L.E.A.D.E.R.S. skills begin with Listening to Learn and end with Speaking with Specificity, indicating the importance of communication to everyday leadership. This chapter will help the sender prepare his or her remarks and make them aligned verbally, vocally, and visually. The content in Chapter 3 on Listening to Learn helps the receiver of a message. The goal of the present chapter is to help the sender speak with dignity, free from affectations or embarrassing mannerisms, and to present a person in balance with all their faculties, confident, convinced of their content, and respectfully conveying the information for the benefit of the listener. Everyday leaders speak specifically for the listener as well as for themselves.

SPEAKING REVEALS LEADERSHIP

Speaking reveals our leadership skills as well as the personal power and sphere of influence one has in an organization. Speaking is an interpersonal skill and has a subset of three skills: the verbal, vocal, and visual elements of our speaking. These three elements, when used by an everyday leader skillfully in a mutually reinforcing way, create a confluence of the verbal, vocal, and visual elements of the message. The confluence of elements helps create credibility for the everyday leader and confidence in the message. Thus, speaking skills, one-to-one or to a small group, have a relationship with our leadership skills. There is no hiding from this reality, and there is no substitute for speaking well. Our daily conversations do have an impact on how well we can practice everyday leadership. The spoken word makes us visible. Speaking reveals our knowledge or lack of it; involves the verbal, vocal, and visual representations of our thinking, feeling, and passions; and demonstrates the value we place on relationships. Speaking demonstrates our integrity and character.

How does speaking impact on a leader's effectiveness? This chapter will address that question with the assumption that it is possible to improve one's speaking specificity in everyday conversations with individuals and with groups. This chapter reveals additional information about speaking in a different context as well—that is, when everyday leaders have to deal with the media.

CONFLUENCE OF THE VERBAL, VOCAL, AND VISUAL ELEMENTS OF SPEAKING

The verbal, vocal, and visual elements of speaking comprise three working parts of conversations involved in everyday leadership. The choice, sequencing, clarity, and delivery of the words used represent the verbal element of speaking. The vocal element refers to the vocal variety of the sound of the words we use. Our facial expressions, smiles, eye contact, gestures, postures, movements, personal space practices, dress, grooming, and appearance of a speech reveal the visual element in conversations. When the three aspects of sending a message in a conversation work in confluence with each other, the understanding of the message intended for shared meaning is enhanced, thereby projecting conviction, confidence, and the credibility of the message.

What is the relationship among these three elements? R. L. Birdwhistell (1970) suggests that 30 to 35 percent of a message is carried by the words and 60 to 65 percent is carried by the vocal and visual elements. John Philpott's research supports Birdwhistell's notions. Philpott found only 31 percent of the meaning was carried by the verbal element. In his work, *Communicating Without Words* (1968), A. Mehrabian reports that only 7 percent of the message is carried by the words, 38 percent is carried by the vocal element, and 55 percent is carried by the visual element of the message. Confluence is critical because if the verbal element of speaking is not aligned with the vocal and visual elements, people will tend to believe only the vocal and visual elements. This could be quite embarrassing if the everyday leader spent most of the time choosing the right words and those words did not align with the vocal and visual elements.

Indeed, the idea that listeners, in attempting to create meaning from a speech, rely more on the vocal and visual elements than the verbal has been established for some time. Speaking face to face, where the three elements are evident, is the richest, most desirable medium for delivering a credible message, followed by telephones, e-mail, personal letters, notes, and memos. In their work, *The Best Guide to Effective Presentations: A Step-by-Step Approach* (1997), J. L. Jankovich and E. A. LeMay suggest that listeners remember 20 percent of what they hear; 30 percent of what they see; and 50 to 85 percent of what they both see and hear.

If an everyday leader speaks well, he or she can elicit attention, relay ideas, provide order and direction, solve problems, persuade, and build trust. To share the meaning of a message is the charge to which an everyday leader commits. If we have listened, understood, enjoyed, and shared in someone's message, the sender has created a shared meaning. A lasting takeaway message from a conversation comes by way of a speaker-designed residual message that emphasizes the message to be shared and retained. Evidence that the residual message carried across from the sender to the receiver successfully comes from the words remembered, the sound of the voice recalled, and the image that lingers in our minds. Preparation goes into an effective conversation. Moreover, if a person wants to be successful in his or her everyday leadership, much has to be developed within the person. Speaking skills need to be honed.

The confluence of the verbal, vocal, and visual elements of speaking skills help an everyday leader lead as the people receiving the message attain clearer understanding. Joint understanding or shared meaning of a message is enhanced by the confluence of the verbal, vocal, and visual elements of speaking, irrespective of the purpose of communication. The everyday leader could be conducting a performance review, interviewing a potential hire, persuading a client, or networking across silos in an organization, or discussing how to approach a problem in the work. In instances of face-to-face communication, the confluence of the three elements of speaking is important. The following survey speaks to the relevance of all three elements of speaking.

SURVEY REPORT

I conducted a survey with 42 managers representing seven professional categories (manufacturing, service, software sales, health care, retail, utilities, and government) regarding the importance of the verbal, vocal, and visual elements of speaking. The reports following represent some of the findings.

1. Regarding the three elements in client relations, one interviewee said, "You only have one opportunity to impress another person. A powerful voice, the right words, and good body language must be used the first time, or there won't be a next time."

2. Regarding a presentation with a select audience, a certified public accountant shared this story. His speaking skills were heavily dependent upon choosing the rights words, keeping the terminology simple while avoiding contradictory statements when speaking. At a tax conference he learned the value of the verbal message as well as the vocal part of the message, when a client in an audience of many potential clients stood up halfway through the talk and said, "I'll be back when you learn to speak English."

3. One female executive interviewed indicated that the girlish quality of her voice was holding her back from a corporate directorship. Her superior often remarked, albeit crudely so, that colleagues would listen more seriously to what she had to say when she stopped "squeaking." Studies indicate that middle to lower tones in the vocal element test better in the boardroom.

4. A contracts manager for a major electronics corporation was directed by his superior to seek speech help because he had difficulty articulating some words. During negotiations his bodily tension caused vocal breathiness and

loss of intensity. This experience weakened his vocal and visual image. He reports that the result was a loss of contracts.

5.   The CEO of a highly visible firm who already possessed a good voice quality expressed concern about his presentation skills, particularly when interacting with the media. The sound of his voice was clear and easy to follow but when he appeared on camera, his image of credibility was crumbled. His posture was stiff and frozen, his eyes shifted nervously, and he looked too serious. His message as a result was questioned and he appeared not credible.

From among these scenarios in the work world, one theme seems to be the ability of discernment. All three elements of speaking, the verbal, vocal, and visual should flow into one another and that if confluent, the three parts come into a seamless, mutually supportive whole presentation of a leader.

THE VERBAL ELEMENT OF SPEAKING

Peter Drucker once said, "One cannot communicate a word without the whole person coming with it" (Drucker, 1974). Our words lead but the vocal and visual trail behind like an entourage leaving an even more powerful message.

A common myth accepted by many is that the verbal choices are what make a good conversation. Usually, the receiver of the message tends to determine meaning more from the vocal and visual cues in conjunction with the verbal aspect. The myth occurs in job interviews and workplace conversations too. The verbal, vocal, and visual elements are critically important for an everyday leader.

When we refer to the verbal element of speaking, we are referring to words and grammar. In 1975, Edgar Dale wrote elegantly of the eight values of words in *The Word Game: Improving Communications*. They are as follows:

1.   Words are for communicating, sharing ideas, and understanding people. We think, work, and play with words.

To develop sensitivity to words is necessary to recognize
and distinguish the visionary's plain speech from the
demagogue's rhetoric.

2. Words are for conceptualizing. Words are written and
   spoken symbols for concepts, which are the distilled
   essence of our tangible and intangible experiences with
   objects and events.

3. Words are for building an active mind capable of distin-
   guishing subtle differences among concepts. An active
   mind readily puts ideas in models, outlines, paradigms,
   frames of reference, categories, matrices, grids, and
   summaries.

4. Words are for filing, retrieving, and reorganizing information. Information not adequately organized and reor-
   ganized for later use will be forgotten. The ability to
   classify information, especially in this age of networked
   societies, can help systematize interrelated particulars
   and the interrelationship of words.

5. Words are for reading. Reading is simply thinking about
   the meaning of words.

6. Words are for speaking and writing. Many specialists
   have not been able to put important technological, economic, political, social, and health-care information into
   interesting, easy-to-understand speech or prose. Great
   speakers and writers communicate not to confuse or con-
   found their listeners, but to share thoughts and feelings.

7. Words help to improve the range and depth of professional and personal experience.

8. Words are for creating metaphors. The word *metaphor*
   comes from *meta,* meaning "across" and *phor,* meaning
   "carry." To create a metaphor in conversation or a
   speech is to carry a meaning across, transfer it, and
   apply it, in a fresh new way.

   The value of words, as emphasized above, can be trans-
lated into a useful checklist of practices that will help an
everyday leader employ the power of words. The seven practices follow.

PRACTICING THE VERBAL ELEMENT OF SPEAKING

WORD CHOICE, MEANING, AND PRONUNCIATION

Choosing the appropriate word is important because of the imprecise nature of language and the varied meaning of words. Improper choices or too many words chosen for the message will cause confusion. Choose words that everyone in the audience will understand. Choose words that you can pronounce correctly. Pronouncing words incorrectly will decrease your credibility with your audience and decrease confidence in yourself. Don't use words out of context. If you give new meaning to an old word, be sure to clarify the change with your audience. Recognize the power of words.

Sentence Arrangement

The proper arrangement of sentences is important too. If thoughts or ideas are out of sequence in your presentation, the audience will not be able to follow the syntax of your message. Different structures of a speech, described below, will help in arranging the grammar and sentences of the talk. Deal with the complexity of language.

Simplified Language

Simplifying the language in a speech helps the speaker to be concise and convincing. A number of experts in this area suggest using an active voice. For example, "We can save the company one million dollars" as opposed to "One million dollars can be saved." Also, using personal language such as personal pronouns is recommended. For example, "Our company" not " The company." Use short words and short sentences because it will help you design a more natural speech.

Vivid Language

Speakers should appeal to the senses by choosing words that visualize your ideas. Use word pictures, metaphors, analogies, and lifelike images to conceptualize and visualize your ideas. Making the language vivid helps the audience retain the message.

Structured Repetition of the Residual Message
Another way to help your audience retain your message is to design into your speech the takeaway message at least three times. Creatively, without saying the exact same sentence each time, reveal the essence of the message once in the introduction of the talk, once or twice in the body of the talk, and once in the conclusion.

AVOID SECRET JARGON LANGUAGE AND EMOTIONAL OVERTONES

Obstacles that prevent us from using words effectively include jargon, slang, technical terms, discriminatory remarks, and gender-specific language. Also, special language or jargon that are meaningful to only a few individuals or to a select group, usually creates an atmosphere of distrust and an "in-group"–"out-group" divisiveness. Discriminatory language should also be avoided, as well as language that does not include everyone in the company. G. N. Toogood (1996) advises that this practice alone will distinguish you from the pack and allow you to become a more credible speaker.

REDUCE NONWORDS AND VOCAL FILLERS

Nonwords and vocal fillers are the sounds we use to fill in perfectly good silences which, if left intact, would help your audience be more attentive to your talk. Nonwords include the use of *ums, ers, ahs,* and similar subvocalizations. Vocal fillers are words that have no value-added to the talk itself. They include words or phrases like *okay, you know,* and *kind of.* Replace these nonwords and vocal fillers with silent pauses, and your audience will appreciate the silence.

SUMMARY CHECKLIST FOR THE VERBAL ELEMENT OF SPEAKING

The verbal element of speaking consists of words and the grammar of their arrangement—what it is that you are saying.

- Vocabulary (list of words from which to choose)

- Word choice
- Word meaning (semantics)
- Word order or sequence
- Clarity of the pronunciation of the words (phonology)
- Sentence arrangement (syntax)
- Simplified language to be concise and convincing
- Vivid language to help conceptualize and visualize ideas
- Use of word pictures, metaphors, analogies, or lifelike images
- Structured repetition of the residual message
- Avoidance of slang, jargon, unnecessary technical terms, discriminatory remarks and gender-specific language
- Reduction of vocal fillers and nonwords (*ums, ahs, ers; okay, you know*—and the like)
- Minimized use of dialects, accents, regionalisms
- Attention to the overall structure of the speech

THE VOCAL ELEMENT OF SPEAKING

Aristotle once remarked that it is not sufficient to know what one ought to put into words, one must also know how to say it. How you vocally use the words you have crafted in the structure of a speech is critical to an everyday leader. How an everyday leader sounds is as important as what he or she is saying. Words are important in speaking for influence and leadership; they should be aligned with the vocal and the visual message. Even though the worth of the words is important, listeners usually weigh the worth of the speech by the voice and visual image of the speaker. The voice and visual elements of a conversation speak to the will of the speaker. The tone of your voice is vital to the consequence of your message considering that much of the hard feelings between people originate from the use of a punishing or threatening tone of voice. This section examines seven practices to improve the vocal element of speaking.

PRACTICING THE VOCAL ELEMENT OF SPEAKING

- *Proper breath support.* Proper breathing while speaking allows the speaker to vary his or her volume, tone, pacing, rate of silences in a speech, and pitch.
- *Proper enunciation.* Avoid dropping the ends of words, mumbling through some words, speaking with a mouth half closed, and trailing off at the end of a sentence. Increase attention and emphasize the movement of your lips, mouth, and jaw muscle while speaking to someone and enunciating the words properly will be easier.
- *Varying volume.* The loudness of your voice is the vehicle upon which your voice is projected. Alter the volume to keep the receiver attentive to your conversation and to draw their attention to a key point in your message.
- *Varying tone.* The tone of your conversation has to do with the intensity and vitality of the resonant sound itself. This tone is influenced by your utmost intention. The intention of your conversation should be noncondescending and as free from bias as possible. A speaker could admit bias but then try to present content in an objective way. Any hint of sarcasm in your voice or negative emotion will be picked up by the receiver and that will often turn them against your content. Sarcasm usually masks anger.
- *Varying the pace of words.* It is believed that the average pace in words per minute for most people who are speaking is 125 words. Listeners, however, can process at least twice as many words per minute. Sometimes, listeners can listen accurately to up to 400 words per minute. Don't be too slow or too fast in your pace if you are a speaker who can speak faster than 125 words per minute. Also, if you alternately speed up and slow down during your conversation, it will likely help keep the receiver attentive to your comments.
- *Varying rate of pauses.* Silence is part of speaking. Silences can be planned within the overall pace of a conversation. The number and length of the pauses in a conversation have

a wonderful effect on the receiver. When a person hears silence, he or she begins to focus their attention on the person speaking. The receiver will remember longer the comments just after a pause than at other times. Thus, the rate of pauses can enhance the power of your words in a conversation. The pauses surround the words and the silences have a voice unto themselves.

- *Varying pitch.* It is suggested that using a monotone voice is to be avoided as it relaxes the listeners away from active listening. A monotone voice is using the same pitch or intonation throughout the talk. Alter the intonation to keep your listener from being bored.

SUMMARY CHECKLIST FOR THE VOCAL ELEMENT OF SPEAKING

VOCAL
This involves what you sound like when you are speaking.

- Breath support for quality of sound
- Breath support for varied projection
- Clarity of the enunciation of the sound of the words (the manner of articulation)
- Volume variety (altering amplitude = loudness and softness)
- Tone variety (altering vitality and intensity/resonance)
- Pace variety (altering speed)
- Rate variety (altering the number and length of silent pauses)
- Pitch variety (altering intonation, the highness or lowness of your voice)

SIX AREAS FOR PERFOMANCE IMPROVEMENT IN THE VOCAL ELEMENT OF YOUR MESSAGE

1. *To improve believability,* alter vocal tone, speak slower, and use downward inflections.
2. *To improve inspiration,* alter pace and use vocal enthusiasm.

3.   *To improve articulation,* maintain proper breath support and use proper pronunciation.

4.   *To eliminate monotone,* alter pitch levels, vary loudness, and vary pace and timing.

5.   *To eliminate nonwords,* practice well, video to become aware, and use pauses.

6.   *To eliminate vocal strain,* practice proper breathing and open chest cavity for full sound release.

THE VISUAL ELEMENT OF SPEAKING

Your appearance is the most important visual aid to your message. You are the central visual aid. Use yourself in your delivery. The visual element of speaking includes facial expressions, eye contact, gestures, posture, physical movement while speaking, appearance, poise, and mannerisms.

PRACTICING THE VISUAL ELEMENT OF SPEAKING

FACIAL EXPRESSIONS

Your facial expressions while speaking can enhance or deter from your credibility and conviction as an everyday leader. The expressions that are reflected when speaking can undermine your message. If you tell your peers that you are happy to talk with them and you keep looking at your watch with an impatient expression on your face during the conversation, you will not be believable. Your overall perception by others will be that you are seen as contradictory to the word you use. The same applies to a deadpan look on your face when delivering good news. It is good to be animated, showing that you can be concerned, excited, and respectful. Smiling is a wonderful facial expression when it matches your words and the content and context of a situation. Smiling, besides projecting a confident image, puts both your facial muscles at ease as well as the person to whom you are speaking and an entire audience. Avoid excessive seriousness, furrowed brow, and noticeable blinking of the eyelids.

EYE CONTACT AND A SMILE

Smiling has other values as well. Smiling, which ranges from a pleasant, happy, or content look to a broad smile, helps connect with the person to whom you are speaking. Your listeners, whether a person or an audience, will become more at ease with a smile as it creates an atmosphere of positive feelings. It is suggested that smiling helps a speaker make eye contact with your listeners and helps the speaker reveal his or her own natural personality during the conversation. Nelson and Wallich (1994) suggest that eye contact is closely linked with your sincerity and the meaning of your message.

In addition, eye contact encourages active listening and allows the speaker to see the feedback from the listeners about their understanding of what is being said. G. N. Toogood (1996) reminds us to really look at the people, not over their heads, at their feet, or at your feet for that matter. Look at the eyeballs of the listeners. Look at them to see them, not just to be able to say you looked their way. If you can't bear to look at their eyes, then at least look at their faces. If you can manage to see them, eyeball to eyeball and nose to nose, you will be with your listeners, not just speaking to them. You may want to blend the eye contact with pauses of silence. In a personal conversation, the eye contact should be more frequent.

GESTURES

Gestures can visually amplify your words. Gestures can always be used for the benefit of listeners of any kind. Vary your gestures using them to help bring attention to important ideas. Leave your arms and hands at your side or in front comfortably positioned when not using gestures. Gestures help diffuse trapped nervous energy in your body when speaking if you are nervous for any reason. If the nervous energy builds up without release, it can cause the everyday leader to look nervous even though psychologically he or she is poised. Gesture should help not hinder the transferring of a message. Sometimes it is good to break the normal sphere within which you gesture. Making a large, grandiose gesture can serve to emphasize an important point of your talk. Good gestures are head nods and hand and arm movement, which emphasizes size, number, and direction. All gestures should accentuate the message and usually come along naturally unless an everyday leader is trying to program them which results in awkwardness.

Gestures can become overbearing and distracting too. A number of experts in the area suggest the following list of things not to do when conversing.

- Don't play with paperclips, pointers, note cards, coins in the pocket, jewelry, key chains, or watches.
- Don't twirl rings or stroke chin or beard
- Don't click pens or play with markers
- Don't twist, fluff hair, or constantly play with the hair
- Don't bite lip, lick lips, or press lips
- Don't have hands in constant motion
- Don't have hands behind back (parade rest or handcuffed)
- Don't hold one arm by the opposite hand (wounded soldier)
- Don't have hands in front of lower extremity (figleaf)
- Don't have arms folded in front of you as it indicates insecurity
- Don't put hands together as if praying (sisters of mercy)
- Don't wring hands or put both hands in your pocket
- Don't drum hands on the podium or table
- Don't fiddle with eyeglasses
- Don't tug or touch nose or ears
- Don't twiddle thumbs
- Don't cover your mouth
- Don't crack the knuckles

Using a videotape is the best way to identify your visual image. If you want to identify your most common gesture, video tape your next conversation with the listener's permission and play it fast forward. Your most commonly used gestures will reveal themselves. The video will help focus attention on the everyday leader's facial expressions, eye contact, posture, physical movement, and general appearance.

POSTURE
Again, a video of yourself speaking is the best way to ascertain what about your posture needs to be changed. A general target for a speaker's posture is to be dignified, comfortable, relaxed, and alert. Avoid a sloppy, rigid, shifting, or excessively swaying posture. Evenly distribute your weight. Determine which stance is best for you with even distribution in mind. Whatever your choice, stand tall.

PHYSICAL MOVEMENT
Both standing in one spot and speaking or moving purposefully is acceptable. If you move, look at the person or persons that are in the direction you are moving. Don't look down and move. Constant moving is to be avoided. At these times be sure not to create too much diversion. If you want the listener to be looking at you, look at the listener. Use physical movement sparingly.

DRESS AND APPEARANCE
Even though there are no universal fashion standards, like it or not, the manner in which you dress does affect how people listen to you. A first impression is hard to erase, so it is wise to plan the first impression you want to create.

HUMOR
Humor can be a tool to help you deliver any message. The best humor is telling stories about yourself as it helps establish rapport with the listener. If you are not comfortable telling stories or using jokes, cartoons work well. Don't use inappropriate, unsuitable, or irrelevant stories. Always tie the humor to your message. Make sure you are comfortable telling the joke or the story. Don't use sarcasm as it leaves a negative impression.

THINGS TO AVOID
- *Facial expressions:* excessive seriousness, furrowing brow, mixed look
- *Eye contact:* glancing or quick peeks at audience or never looking at them
- *Gestures:* fiddling with hair, eyeglasses, pens, or paper

- *Posture:* slouching the shoulders and a frozen posture
- Physical movement: nervous pacing

THINGS TO REMEMBER

- *Facial expressions:* relax facial muscles and match expressions to content of message
- *Eye contact:* look at audience members, hold the gaze for 2 to 3 seconds, be sincere
- *Gestures:* use the gesture that naturally emphasizes your word
- *Posture:* stand tall but not stiff
- *Physical movement:* moving is okay if it is natural as movement helps keep attention
- *Poise:* comes about from practice, practice, and more practice

SUMMARY CHECKLIST FOR THE VISUAL ELEMENT OF SPEAKING

VISUAL (IMAGE, BODY LANGUAGE, AND POISE—WHAT YOU LOOK LIKE WHEN YOU ARE SPEAKING)

- Facial expressions (animate = smile, concerned, excited, respectful; avoid deadpan)
- Eye contact (engage everyone's eyes in the audience if possible)
- Gestures (use hands, arms, stance, and so on, to naturally accentuate; avoid distracting gestures)
- Posture (stand tall within and on outside; avoid stiffness, shrugging, or slouching the shoulders)
- Physical movement (some walking is okay, but avoid pacing, swaying, rocking, and shifting)
- Dress, groom, and appear as appropriate for the situation (avoid styles that consume attention)
- Poise (visible composure, assurance, and dignity of manner in the bearing or deportment of the head and body

that signals an unflappable equilibrium; avoid affected
and embarrassing mannerisms)

GENERAL GUIDELINES FOR HOLDING ATTENTION
OF LISTENERS

1. Start with the conclusion so they know where you are
    taking them. You lose them if you lead up to your main
    idea.
2. Translate the benefits to the listener as soon as possible
    and do it often.
3. Use examples to repeat your point without boring them.
4. Use specific conversation not generalized conversation.
5. Ask questions of the listener to gage their understand-
    ing.
6. Avoid too many details.
7. Never over estimate the amount of knowledge or infor-
    mation people possess.
8. There are many meanings of words; be sure your mean-
    ing is the meaning that is being picked up by the other
    person.
9. Speaking and listening demands the cooperation of both
    speaker and listener and both should be aware of this
    duty. This approach helps to maintain the empathy of
    emotion in a positive mood. This in turn clears the way
    for responsiveness.

WHEN EVERYDAY LEADERS HAVE TO DEAL
WITH THE MEDIA

G. N. Toogood (1996) reports that many people polled distrust
TV reporters and often refuse to be interviewed. Yet television
is an opportunity as well as a risk. Handled well, it can be of
benefit to your company. The following suggestions should
help in dealing with the media.

1. Consider yourself being interviewed from the first contact on the telephone or e-mail message. If you discuss what is not to be covered it welcomes more questions and the content to be left out usually becomes a key point.
2. Care more about the message you want to leave behind than if you are being successful as an interviewee.
3. Know the interviewer, the host in many cases. Know the format of the interview or the show. Know the outcome of other shows or interviews. Know if the purpose is style for ratings or substance for delivering information.
4. Attempt to be positive, helpful, and enthusiastic in your clarification and instruction. Give vivid examples.
5. Attack not the competition nor an opponent, especially since they are not there to defend themselves. It is acceptable to question logic or reasoning. It is not preferred to attack someone's character or motives. Attacks usually turn on the attacker.
6. Avoid jargon or secret language. Be as helpful as you can to explain clearly what you know and what you do not know.
7. Listen carefully and avoid reacting to loaded questions based on false or hostile intentions.
8. Be yourself but be alert.
9. Plan your quotable quotes well in advance of the interview. Use them like the residual message of the interview. These can be quotes that become clever phrases that grab the attention of the viewers of the interview.
10. Use statistics to add credibility but be careful not to clutter the message.
11. Use your own experience if it was something you have personally met with and have eyewitness recollections.
12. Defuse loaded questions by (a) disagreeing with the loaded premise (I do not agree with that characterization of the problem); (b) recognizing that some people agree with the loaded premise (it may be true that some

people believe that); or (c) bridging immediately to your position (it may be true for some people but they may fail to recognize…).

13. Don't be afraid to say that you changed your way of looking at something over time. A change of heart can signal flexibility and open-mindedness. Explain why too.

14. Microphones are always on in the studio. If they are not, then it is a good thing to be wrong about and you haven't inadvertently given information that can be used out of context.

15. Nod your head only in agreement, not out of courteousness to the questioner. A visual head nod sends the signal of agreeing, and if the question is controversial, the head nod might not communicate your intentions.

16. If you are in a hot room, wipe your brow with your finger, not a handkerchief. Again the visual of wiping your brow with a handkerchief looks like they are making you sweat.

17. Keep your eye on the host or the other panelists, not the "on" camera. If you do play to the camera, you may look distracted or like you are just plain grandstanding.

18. Try not to look at yourself in the TV monitor. Again, stay in the action of the exchange of information not on how good you may look on camera.

19. Be likeable, be prepared with facts and figures, and stay poised if attacked.

20. Try to be concise and short. Usually 80 words or less or 18 seconds is about the average time on a clip. Bridge to your points quickly.

EPILOGUE

In summary, the L.E.A.D.E.R.S. Method is a roadmap readers can use to hone and practice leadership skills every day. Being able to understand your own motivations, emotional responses, and practical goals are critical to fully using the L. E.A.D.E.R.S. Method. Applying the L.E.A.D.E.R.S. Method requires that you engage the other person with your rational mind, leaving aside personal or emotional agendas. This ability to manage the flow of your emotions, moods, and ego during an exchange is the foundation for authentic communication. The method thus becomes a powerful tool, embodying a combination of competencies which can be used in everyday interactions, from formal meetings to the smallest of conversations. Leaving your ego and emotions at the door ensures that your position as a leader is perceived as authentic and genuine; in turn this instills great confidence in your own leadership abilities.

If people at all levels of an organization practice these skills, then you have leadership in conversation being practiced at all levels and all departments of the organization. Management is easier when leadership abides throughout the organization and when individuals choose to use his/her territory of influence in a positive way. These essential skills, when practiced, allow the person to bring to their territory of influence greater productivity, meaningfulness at work and enjoyment. This results in a culture of learning where people can be excited about going to their place of employment because they are developing their repertoire of leadership skills. This allows leaders to develop earlier in their careers rather than wait until they ascend to a managerial post. The seven essential skills, as depicted in the L.E.A.D.E.R.S. Method, make up the fundamental skill base from which a leader can draw upon at every stage of their career. They are, in fact, the first essential skills in leadership.

CONVERSATION SKILLS FOR EVERYDAY LEADERS

Please rank your level of need for each of the following items ranging from **"0"** (Not of Current Concern), **"1"** (Somewhat Relevant), **"2"** (Moderately Relevant), **"3"** (Primarily Relevant), or **"4"** (Requires Immediate Attention). Please circle the number for each item, indicating your preference.

VERBAL (Words)					
Word Choice	0	1	2	3	4
Pronunciation	0	1	2	3	4
Sentence	0	1	2	3	4
Arrangement	0	1	2	3	4
Simplified Language	0	1	2	3	4
Vivid Language	0	1	2	3	4
Avoids Jargon	0	1	2	3	4
Few Nonwords / Fillers	0	1	2	3	4

VOCAL (Sounds)

Proper Breath Support	0	1	2	3	4
Articulation	0	1	2	3	4
Volume Variety	0	1	2	3	4
Tone Variety	0	1	2	3	4
Pace of Words	0	1	2	3	4
Use of Silences	0	1	2	3	4

VISUAL (Image)

Facial Expressions	0	1	2	3	4
Eye Contact	0	1	2	3	4
Gestures	0	1	2	3	4
Posture	0	1	2	3	4
Physical Movement	0	1	2	3	4
Few Distracting Mannerisms	0	1	2	3	4

STRUCTURE

Purpose Clearly Stated	0	1	2	3	4
Evidence for Main Ideas	0	1	2	3	4
Transitions Between Ideas	0	1	2	3	4
Residual Ideas Repeated	0	1	2	3	4
Recommendations Are Clear	0	1	2	3	4

GENERAL

Nervousness	0	1	2	3	4
Appearance	0	1	2	3	4
Poise/Presence	0	1	2	3	4

BIBLIOGRAPHY

INTRODUCTION

Badaracco, Joseph. *Leading Quietly*. HBS Press: Boston, 2002.

Goleman, Daniel; Boyatzis, Richard; McKee, Annie. *Primal Leadership: Realizing the Power of Emotional Intelligence.* HBS Press: Boston, 2002.

Useem, Michael. *Leading Up: How to Lead Your Boss So You Both Win.* Crown Business: New York, 2001.

CHAPTER 1

Brouwer, Paul. "The Power to See Ourselves." *Harvard Business Review*, November 1, 1964.

Dean, Peter J. "A Critical Incident Study Investigating the Perceived Effective and Ineffective Leadership Behaviors of Iowa Community College Presidents." Ph.D. Dissertation, The University of Iowa, Iowa City, Iowa, 1986.

Dean, Peter J. "Leadership, Leaders and Leading: Part One, Two, and Three." *Performance Improvement Quarterly*, 2002, 15(1), 5–11; 15(2), 3–16; 15(1), 3–11.

Duska, Ron. *Personal Conversations.* The American College: Bryn Mawr, PA, 2005.

Huddleston, M.W. "The Future of the SES." *Government Executive,* February 2000, 32 (2), 76.

CHAPTER 2

Abramson, M.A.; Clyburn, S.; Mercier, E. *Comparing the Pay and Benefits of Federal and Nonfederal Executives.* U.S. Government Printing Office: Washington, DC, 1999.

Banville, T.G. *How to Listen—How to Be Heard.* Nelson-Hall: Chicago, 1978.

Bergmann, Horst; Jurson, Kathleeen; Russ-Eft, Darlene. *Everyone a Leader.* John Wiley & Sons: New York, 1999.

Csikszentmihalyi, M. *Flow: The Experience of Optimal Experience.* HarperCollins Publishers: New York, 1990.

Davis, Keith. *Human Relations in Business.* McGraw Hill: New York, 1957.

Devine, T.G. "Listening: What We Know after Fifty Years of Research and Theorizing. *Journal of Reading,* 1978, 21, 296–304.

Greenleaf, Robert K. *Servant Leadership: A Journey into the Nature of Legitimate Power and Greatness.* Paulist Press: Mahwah, NJ, 1977.

Heifetz, Ronald A. *Leadership without Easy Answers.* Belknap Press of Harvard University Press: Cambridge, MA, 1998.

Hunter, James C. *The World's Most Powerful Leadership Principles.* Random House: New York, 2005.

Kouzes, James M.; Posner, Barry Z. *The Leadership Challenge.* Jossey-Bass: San Francisco, 2002.

Morris, T. *True Success: A New Philosophy of Excellence.* Berkley Books: New York, 1994.

Rogers, C. *A Way of Being.* Houghton Mifflin: Boston, 1980.

Zenger, John; Folkman, Joseph. *Handbook for Leaders: 24 Lessons for Extraordinary Leaders.* McGraw Hill: New York, 2005.

CHAPTER 3

Csikszentmihalyi, M. *Flow: The Experience of Optimal Experience.* HarperCollins Publishers: New York, 1990.

Davis, Keith. *Human Relations in Business.* McGraw Hill: New York, 1957.

Greenleaf, Robert K. *Servant Leadership: A Journey into the Nature of Legitimate Power and Greatness.* Paulist Press: Mahwah, NJ, 1977.

Hunter, James C. *The World's Most Powerful Leadership Principles.* Random House: New York, 2005.

Listening Skills—How to Be an Active Listener; 160-frame, color, 2x2 slides-record-cassette-script. Center for Humanities, Inc.: White Plains, NY, 1977.

Nuer, L. "Learning as Leadership." Personal correspondence, 1998, PO Box 728, Larkspur, CA 94977.

Okun, S.K. "How to Be a Better Listener." *Nation's Business,* 1975, 63, 59–60.

Rogers, C. *A Way of Being.* Houghton Mifflin: Boston, 1980.

The Power of Listening. 16-mm color film. McGraw-Hill: Del Mar, CA, 1978. 26 minutes.

Zenger, John; Folkman, Joseph. *Handbook for Leaders: 24 Lessons for Extraordinary Leaders.* McGraw Hill: New York, 2005.

CHAPTER 4

Bellah, R. N.; Madsen, R.; Sullivan, W. M.; Swidler, A.; Tipton, S. M. *Habits of the Heart.* University of California Press: Los Angeles, 1985.

Goleman, Daniel. *Emotional Intelligence.* Bantam Books: New York, 1995.

Goleman, Daniel. *Working with Emotional Intelligence.* Bantam Books: New York, 1998.

Goleman, Daniel; Boyatzis, Richard; McKee, Annie. *Primal Leadership: Realizing the Power of Emotional Intelligence.* HBS Press: Boston, 2002.

Goleman, T. B. *Emotional Alchemy: How the Mind Can Heal the Heart.* Three Rivers Press: New York, 2001.

Greenberg, H.; Weinstein, H.; Sweeney, P. *How to Hire and Develop Your Next Top Performer: The Five Qualities That Make Salespeople Great.* McGraw-Hill: New York, 2001.

Segal, Morley. *Points of Influence: A Guide to Using Personality Theory.* Jossey-Bass: San Francisco, 1997.

CHAPTER 5

Dean, Peter J. "A Qualitative Method of Assessment and Analysis for Changing Organizational Culture." *Performance Improvement Journal,* 1998, 37 (2), ISPI Publications: Silver Spring, MD.

Erikson, E. "Identity and the Life Cycle." *Psychological Issues,* 1959, 1 (1). International Universities Press: New York. Found in Atkins, S. *The Name of the Game.* Ellis & Stewart Publishers: Beverly Hills, CA, 1981.

Freud, S. *The Standard Edition of the Complete Psychological Works of Sigmund Freud.* Hogarth Press and Institute of Psycho-Analysis: London, 1963; Vol. 16, Part III: *Introductory Lectures on Psycho-Analysis* (J. Strachey, ed.). (Originally published 1917.)

Fromm, E. *Escape from Freedom.* Farrar & Reinhart: New York, 1941. In Atkins, S. *The Name of the Game.* Ellis & Stewart Publishers: Beverly Hills, CA, 1981.

Goleman, Daniel; Boyatzis, Richard; McKee, Annie. *Primal Leadership: Realizing the Power of Emotional Intelligence.* HBS Press: Boston, 2002.

Gilley, J. W.; Dean, P. J.; Bierema, L. *Philosophy and Practice of Organizational Learning, Performance, and Change.* Perseus Publishing: Cambridge, MA, 2001.

Horney, K. *Neurosis and Human Growth: The Struggle Toward Self-Realization.* W. W. Norton: New York, 1950.

Isaac, Robert G.; Zerbe, Wilfred J.; Pitt, Douglas C. "Leadership and Motivation: The Effective Application of Expectancy Theory." *Journal of Managerial Issues*, 2001, 13(2), 212–227.

James, William. *Talks to Teachers on Psychology and to Students on Life's Ideals* (1899). Reprint. Harvard University Press: Cambridge, MA, 1983.

Jung, C. G. *Man and His Symbols.* Doubleday: New York, 1964.

Lewin, K. et al. "The Practicality of Democracy." In *Human Nature and Enduring Peace;* G. Murphy, ed. Houghton-Mifflin: Boston, 1945.

Lewin, K. "Frontiers in Group Dynamics, Part 1: Concept, Method and Reality in Social Science: Social Equilibria and Social Change." *Human Relations*, 1947a, 1, 5–41.

Lewin, K. "Frontiers in Group Dynamics, Part 1: Channels of Group life: Social Planning and Action Research." *Human Relations*, 1947b, 1, 143–153.

Lewin, K. "Cultural Reconstruction." In *Resolving Social Conflicts: Selected Papers on Group Dynamics*: G. Lewin, ed. HarperCollins: New York, 1948, 34–42.

Maslow, Abraham H. "A Theory of Human Motivation." *Psychological Review*, 1943, 50, 370–396.

Maslow, Abraham H. *The Far Reaches of Human Nature.* Viking Press: New York, 1971. Cited in Atkins, S. *The Name of the Game.* Ellis & Stewart Publishers: Beverly Hills, CA, 1981.

Maslow, Abraham H. *Maslow on Management.* John Wiley & Sons: New York, 1998.

McDonald, Bob; Hutchenson, Donald. *Don't Waste Your Talent.* Longstreet Press: Atlanta, 2000.

McGregor, D. *The Human Side of Enterprise.* McGraw-Hill: New York, 1960, 46.

Piaget, J. *Jean Piaget: The Man and His Ideas.* Norton: New York, 1973.

Porter, L.; Lawler, E. *Managerial Attitudes and Performance.* Richard D. Irwin: Homewood, IL, 1968.

Rogers, C. R. "A Theory of Therapy, Personality and Interpersonal Relationships, as Developed in the Client-Centered Framework." In *Psychology: A Study of a Science*; S. Koch, ed.; McGraw Hill: New York, 1959; Vol. 3, 184–256.

Vroom, V. H.; Yetton, P. *Leadership and Decision Making.* University of Pittsburgh Press: Pittsburgh, 1973.

CHAPTER 6

Argyris, C.; Schon, D.A. *Organizational Learning: A Theory of Action Perspective.* Addison-Wesley: Reading, 1980.

Argyris, C. *Reasoning, Learning, and Action: Individual and Organizational.* Jossey-Bass: San Francisco, 1982.

Argyris, C. *Knowledge for Action: A Guide to Overcoming Barriers to Organizational Change.* Jossey-Bass: San Francisco, 1993.

Axelrod, D. "Getting Everyone Involved: How One Organization Involved Its Employees, Supervisors, and Managers in Redesigning the Organization." *Journal of Applied Behavioral Science*, 1992, 28 (4), 499–509.

Dean, Peter J. *Guidelines for the Implementation of Change by a Change Team.* Unpublished manuscript, The University of Iowa, Iowa City, Iowa, 1983.

Dean, Peter J.; Dean, M. R.; Guman, E. "Identifying a Range of Performance Improvement Solutions—High Yield Training to Systems Redesign." *Performance Improvement Quarterly*, 1992, 5 (4).

Dean, Peter J. *Re-Engineering the Business Enterprise by Organizational Redesign.* Unpublished manuscript, The Penn State University Press, Great Valley, PA, 1993.

Dean, Peter J. "Examining the Practice of Human Performance Technology." *Performance Improvement Quarterly*, 1995, 8 (2), 68–94.

Dean, Peter J. *Performance Engineering at Work.* International Board of Standards for Training, Performance, and Instruction, IBSTPI Publications and International Society for Performance Improvement: Washington, DC, 1999.

Dean, Peter J.; Ripley, David E. *Performance Improvement Pathfinders: Models for Organizational Learning Systems.* International Society for Performance Improvement Publications: Washington, DC, 1997.

Dean, Peter J.; Blevins, S.; Snodgrass, P. J. "Performance Analysis: An HRD Tool That Drives Change in Organizations." In *In Action: Leading Organizational Change;* Phillips, J.J., Holton III, E.F., eds.. American Society for Training and Development: Alexandria, VA, 1997.

Dean, Peter J.; Ripley, David E. "Instructional Design and Training." In *Performance Improvement Interventions: Methods for Organizational Learning.* International Society of Performance Improvement: Washington, DC, 1998a, Vol. 2.

Dean, Peter J.; Ripley, David E. "Performance Technologies in the Workplace." In *Performance Improvement Interventions: Methods for Organizational Learning.* International Society of Performance Improvement: Washington, DC, 1998b, Vol. 3.

Dean, Peter J.; Ripley, David E. "Culture and Systems Change." In *Performance Improvement Interventions: Methods for Organizational Learning.* International Society of Performance Improvement: Washington, DC, 1998c, Vol. 4.

CHAPTER 7

Beauchamp, T. L.; Bowie, N. E. *Ethical Theory and Business*, 3rd ed. Prentice-Hall: Englewood Cliffs, NJ, 1988.

Bentham, J. *An Introduction to the Principle of Morals and Legislation.* Athlone Press: London, 1979.

Berenbeim, R. E. *Corporate Ethics* (Research Report 900). The Conference Board: New York, 1987.

Brady, F. N. *Ethical Managing: Rules and Results.* Macmillan: New York, 1990.

Dean, Peter J. "Making Codes of Ethics 'Real.'" *Journal of Business Ethics,* 1992, 11(4), 285–291.

Dean, Peter J. "A Selected Review of the Underpinnings of Ethics for Human Performance Technology Professionals," Part 1 and 2. *Performance Improvement Quarterly,* 1993, 6 (4), 3–49.

Dean, Peter J. "Some Basics About Ethics." *Performance and Instruction,* February 1994, 36–45, 49; Spring 1994, 87–96.

Dean, Peter J. "Customizing Codes of Ethics to Set Professional Standards." *Performance Improvement Journal,* 1994, 33 (1).

Dean, Peter J. *Performance Engineering at Work.* ISPI Publications: Silver Spring, MD, 1999.

Dean, Peter J. "Setting Standards for Right and Wrong." *Financial Times,* October 15, 2001.

Dean, Peter J.; Ripley, David E. *Performance Improvement Pathfinders: Models for Organizational Learning Systems.* ISPI Publications: Silver Spring, MD, 1997.

Dean, Peter J. et al. *Academy of Human Resource Development: Standards on Ethics and Integrity.* Academy of Human Resource Development: Baton Rouge, LA, 1999.

Donaldson, Thomas. *Corporations and Morality.* Englewood Cliffs, NJ: Prentice-Hall, 1982.

Donaldson, Thomas. *The Ethics of International Business.* Oxford University Press: New York, 1989.

Donaldson, Thomas. "Values in Tension: Ethics Away from Home." *Harvard Business Review.* September-October 1996.

Donaldson, Thomas; Dunfee, Thomas. "Toward a Unified Conception of Business Ethics: Integrative Social Contract Theory." *Academy of Management Review*, 1994, 19 (2), 279.

Friedman, Milton. "Can a Corporation Have a Conscience?" *New York Times Magazine*, 1970.

Gilley, J. W.; Dean, P. J.; Bierema, L. *Philosophy and Practice of Organizational Learning, Performance, and Change*. Perseus Publishing: Cambridge, MA, 2001.

Harvard Business School Case Number 9-292-114, Salomon and the Treasury Securities Auction.

Harvard Business School Case Number 9-394-009, Sears Auto Centers (A).

Hughes, R. L.; Ginnett, R. C.; Curphy, G. J. *Leadership: Enhancing the Lessons of Experience*. Irwin/McGraw-Hill: New York, 1996.

Kant, I. *The Metaphysical Elements of Justice* (1785; J. Ladd, trans.). New York, NY: Library of Liberal Arts: New York, 1965.

McLagan, P. W. *The Age of Participation: New Governance and the Workplace*. Publishers Group West: Berkeley, CA, 1977.

Mill, J. S. *Utilitarianism*. Bobbs-Merrill: Indianapolis, 1957.

Paine, L. S. "Managing for Organizational Integrity." *Harvard Business Review*, March-April, 1994, Cambridge, MA.

Practice and Teaching Workshop: Colorado Springs, CO, July 1992.

Shaw, W.; Barry, V. *Moral Issues in Business*, 4th Ed. Wadsworth: Belmont, CA, 1989.

Smith, A. *Essays Philosophical and Literary*. Ward, Lock, & Co.: London, 1759.

Smith, A. *The Wealth of Nations* (1776). New York: The Modern Library, 1937.

Werhane, P. H. *Corporate Moral and Social Responsibility*. Unpublished paper presented at a Society for Business Ethics Annual Meeting.

Westgaard, O. *A Credo for Performance Technologists.* International Board of Standards for Training, Performance, and Instruction: Western Springs, IL, 1988.

CHAPTER 8

Ackoff, R. L.; Emery, F. E. *On Purposeful Systems.* Tavistock: London, 1972.

Allport, G. W. *The Nature of Prejudice.* Addison-Wesley: Cambridge, MA, 1954.

Atkins, S. *LIFO Training Manual.* Stuart Atkins, Inc.; Beverly Hills Publishers: Beverly Hills, CA, 1980.

Atkins, S. *The Name of the Game.* Ellis & Stewart: Beverly Hills, CA, 1981.

Block, P. *Flawless Consulting: A Guide to Getting your Expertise Used.* Learning Concepts: Austin, TX, 1981.

Block, P. *Stewardship.* Berrett Koehler Publishers: San Francisco, 1996.

Carkhoff, R. R. *The Exemplar: The Exemplary Performer in the Age of Productivity.* Amherst, MA: HRD Press, 1984.

Collins, J. "Good to Great: Why Some Companies Make the Leap...and Others Don't." Harper Business: New York, 2001.

Emery, F. E.; Emery M. *A Choice of Futures.* Martinus Nijhoff Social Sciences Division, Centre for Continuing Education, ANU: Canberra, 1976.

Emery, F. E.; Thorsdrud, E. *Democracy at Work.* Martinus Nijhoff Social Sciences Division, Centre for Continuing Education, ANU: Canberra, 1976.

Erikson, E. Identity and the Life Cycle. *Psychological Issues,* 1959, 1 (1), International Universities Press: New York. In Atkins, S. *The Name of the Game.* Ellis & Stewart Publishers: Beverly Hills, CA, 1981.

Freud, S. *The Standard Edition of the Complete Psychological Works of Sigmund Freud.* Hogarth Press and Institute of Psycho-

Analysis: London, 1963; Vol. 16, Part III: *Introductory Lectures on Psycho-Analysis* (J. Strachey, ed.). Originally published in 1917.

Fromm, E. *Escape from Freedom*. Farrar & Reinhart: New York, 1941. In Atkins, S. *The Name of the Game*. Ellis & Stewart Publishers: Beverly Hills, CA, 1981.

Geier, J. G. Interpretive Introduction. In Marston, W. M. *Emotions of Normal People*. Persona Press: Minneapolis, MN, 1979.

Greenberg, H.; Weinstein, H.; Sweeney, P. *How to Hire and Develop Your Next Top Performer: The Five Qualities That Make Salespeople Great*. New York: McGraw-Hill, 2001.

Greenleaf, Robert K. *Servant Leadership: A Journey into the Nature of Legitimate Power and Greatness*. Paulist Press: Mahwah, NJ, 1977.

Herzberg, F. *Work and the Nature of Man*. World Publishing: New York, 1966.

James, W. *Talks to Teachers on Psychology and to Students on Life's Ideals*. W.W. Norton & Company: New York, 1958.

Jung, C. G. *Man and His Symbols*. Doubleday: New York, 1964.

Kaplan, S. J.; Kaplan, B. E. *A Study of the Validity of the Personal Profile System*. Kaplan Associates: Chevy Chase, MD and Performax Systems International, Inc.: Minneapolis, MN, 1983.

Kouzes, James M.; Posner, Barry Z. *The Leadership Challenge*. Jossey-Bass: San Francisco, 2002.

Lewin, K.; Lippitt, R.; White, R. "Patterns of Aggressive Behavior in Experimentally Created Social Climates." *Journal of Social Psychology*, 1939, 10, 271–279.

Maccoby, M. "Narcissistic Leaders: The Incredible Pros, the Inevitable Cons." *Harvard Business Review*. January/February 2000, 69–77.

Marston, W. M. *Emotions of Normal People*. Harcourt, Brace Co.: New York, 1928.

Maslow, A. *The Far Reaches of Human Nature.* Viking Press: New York, 1971. In Atkins, S. *The Name of the Game.* Ellis & Stewart Publishers: Beverly Hills, CA

McKee, Annie; Schor, Susan. "Confronting Prejudice and Stereotypes: A Teaching Model." *Performance Improvement Quarterly,* 1999, 12 (1), 181–199.

Nelson, R. B.; Wallick, J. *The Presentation Primer: Getting Your Points Across.* New York: Irwin Professional Publishing, 1994.

Personal Profile System. Performax Systems International, Inc.: Minneapolis, MN, 1985.

Reich, W. *Character Analysis.* Orgone Institute Press: New York, 1949. In Atkins, S. *The Name of the Game.* Ellis & Stewart Publishers: Beverly Hills, CA, 1981.

Rogers, C. R. *Client-Centered Therapy: Its Current Practice, Implication, and Theory.* Houghton Mifflin: Boston, 1951.

Rogers, C. R. "A Theory of Therapy, Personality and Interpersonal Relationships, as Developed in the Client-Centered Framework." In S. Koch, *Psychology: A Study of a Science.* McGraw Hill: New York, 1959; Chapter 3, 184–256.

Rogers, C. *Psychology: A Study of Science,* Vol. 3, *Formulation of the Person and the Social Context;* Koch, Sigmund, Ed.; McGraw-Hill, New York, 1959. Found in Atkins, S. *The Name of the Game.* Ellis & Stewart Publishers: Beverly Hills, CA, 1981.

Senge, P. M. *The Fifth Discipline: The Art and Practice of the Learning Organization.* Doubleday: New York, 1990.

Toogood, G. N. *The Articulate Executive: Learn to Look, Act, and Sound Like a Leader.* New York: McGraw-Hill, 1996.

Zigarmi, Drea; Blanchard, Ken; O'Connor, Michael; Edeburn, Carl. *The Leader Within: Learning Enough about Yourself to Lead Others.* Prentice-Hall: Englewood Cliffs, NJ, 2005.

CHAPTER 9

Archer, D.; Akert, R. M. "Words and Everything Else: Verbal and Nonverbal Cue in Social Interpretation." *Journal of Personality and Social Psychology*, 1977, 26, 443–449.

Birdwhistell, R. L. *Kinetics and Content: Essays on Body Motion Communication.* University of Pennsylvania Press: Philadelphia, 1970, 158.

Britton, J. *The Development of Writing Abilities (11–18).* Heinemann: London, 1975; Urbana, IL: National Council of Teachers of English, 1977.

Burgoon, J. K. "Nonverbal Signals." In *Handbook of Interpersonal Communication.* Knapp, M. L.; Miller, G.R., eds.; Sage Publications: Beverly Hills, CA, 1985; 83–85.

Dale, E. *The Word Game: Improving Communications.* Phi Delta Kappa Educational Foundation Fastback: Bloomington, IN, 1975.

Dean, P. J.; Brooke, J. K.; Shields, L. B. "Examining the Skills of Speaking for Shared Meaning." *Performance Improvement Journal*, July 1996, 35 (6).

Drucker, P. "What Communication Means." *Management: Tasks, Responsibilities, Practice.* Harper & Row: New York, 1974.

Graham, P. *Mary Parker Follett: The Prophet of Management.* Harvard Business School Press: Boston, 1995.

Hanson, G. A.; Hanson, R. T.; Stoddard, T. D. *Say It Right: Guide to Effective Oral Business Presentations.* Irwin Professional Publishing: Chicago, 1995.

Jankovich, J. L.; LeMay, E.A. *The Best Guide to Effective Presentations: A Step-by-Step Approach.* College Customs Series; McGraw-Hill: New York, 1997.

Klepper, M. M. *I'd Rather Die Than Give a Speech: A Comprehensive Guide for Public Speaking.* Irwin Professional Publishing: Chicago, 1994.

Mandel, S. *Effective Presentation Skills: A Practical Guide to Better Speaking.* Crisp Learning: Menlo Park, CA, 2000.

Mehrabian, A. "Communicating without Words." *Psychology Today,* 1968, 52–55.

Mehrabian, A. *Silent Messages.* Wadsworth: Belmont, CA, 75–80.

Nelson, R. B.; Wallick, J. *The Presentation Primer: Getting Your Points Across.* New York: Irwin Professional Publishing, 1994.

Seay, T. A.; Altefruse, M. K. "Verbal and Nonverbal Behavior in Judgments of Facilitative Conditions." *Journal of Counseling Psychology,* 1979, 26, 108–119.

Shields, L. *The Voice That Means Business.* Liberty Publishing Group: NC, 2002.

Tepper, D. T.; Hasse, R. F. "Verbal and Nonverbal Communication of Facilitative Condictions." *Journal of Counseling Psychology,* 1978, 25, 35–44.

Toogood, G. N. *The Articulate Executive: Learn to Look, Act, and Sound Like a Leader.* New York: McGraw-Hill, 1996.

Zelazny, G. *Say It with Presentations: How to Design and Deliver Successful Business Presentations.* New York: McGraw-Hill, 2000.

Index

About the Author

Peter J. Dean, Ph.D., holds the O. Alfred Granum Chair in Management at The American College, where he is an award-winning associate professor of management and leadership. The author of numerous papers and the recipient of several awards for teaching excellence from Wharton and Penn State, among others, Dean is an active consultant who has worked with such companies as Rockwell International, DuPont, Motorola, Sprint, and Johnson & Johnson.